M538
:al-bound with Two CDs

PLAY AND TEACH PERCUSSION

A COLLEGE METHOD FOR SUCCESS IN THE CLASSROOM
A LIFETIME REFERENCE FOR MUSIC TEACHERS

STEVE HOUGHTON AND LINDA PETERSEN

GIA Publications, Inc. • Chicago
www.giamusic.com

These individuals shared their ideas to help create this book, and I wish to thank them for their expertise, passion, and feedback:

John King
Neil Grover
Bob Breithaupt
Rubén Alvarez
Susan Tariq
Kristen Shiner McGuire
Jeff Crowell
Shawn LaFrenz
J. C. Combs
Johnny Lee Lane

These individuals provided production support, and I wish to thank them for their ideas, organizational skills, and efforts:

Linda Petersen - Co-author and Editor
Jim Froseth - *Do It!* Co-author
Mike Nevin - Marching Percussion Section
David Collier - Mallet Section Notes
Todd Schroeder - CD Compilation
Talley Sherwood - CD Recording and Mastering
Devin Keane - Illustrations
James Dean - Cover Art

The professional musicians featured on both CDs are:

Steve Houghton - Drums and Percussion
Tom Warrington - Bass
Paul Viapiano - Guitar
Rich Ruttenburg - Piano
Brian Kilgore - Percussion

- Steve Houghton

ISBN: 978-1-57999-308-7

Copyright © 2004 GIA Publications, Inc.
7404 S. Mason Ave.
Chicago, IL 60638
www.giamusic.com
1-800-442-1358

Table of Contents

Preface

The purpose of this method is to provide the future or current teacher with a concise, practical, hands-on guide to teaching and understanding percussion, and assessment tools. Basic snare drum technique is introduced using rudiments and play-along tracks with models and accompaniments. Keyboard mallet technique is also covered with audio modeling of bells, vibes, xylophone and marimba. Extensive percussion ensembles are included, providing a real-life "in the trenches" experience. Drumset concepts are introduced along with timpani fundamentals. The extensive world percussion chapter highlights African, Brazilian and Afro-Cuban drumming techniques with effective ensembles and modeling.

The entire concert percussion family is also covered with detailed drawings, instructions, audio modeling, and reinforcement exercises: concert bass drum, suspended cymbal, hand cymbals, triangle, woodblock, tambourine, temple blocks, castanets, maracas, finger cymbals, claves, etc. A special marching percussion supplement is included in the Resources Section to provide the teacher with some basic knowledge and performance exercises for the marching drum line. The Resources Section also includes a percussion manufacturers list, stick and mallet suggestions, method book suggestions, percussion publishers list, and world percussion instrument guide. These materials will help the director develop a broad understanding of the world of beginning percussion.

NOTE: Most of the music in this book, written and recorded, is from *Do It! Play Percussion* – Books 1 & 2 by Steve Houghton from the Band Series *Do It!* by James Froseth used with permission from GIA Publishing.

CD Models/Play-Alongs

A teacher must take advantage of sound modeling at all levels. Play-along CDs are the ultimate teaching tool and have replaced the soundless band method books of old, which were often practiced to a metronome.

The enclosed CDs provide the player/teacher with a wide assortment of valuable information which will be used frequently throughout a music teaching career. On CD#1, the essential rudiments are demonstrated in the proper practicing format. Certain snare drum rudiments will be performed, as well as a variety of excerpts featuring all of the concert percussion instruments introduced in the book. CD#2 features basic drumset beats to greatly assist the player/teacher to develop four-way coordination skills using a systematic, successful approach. Jazz, rock and Latin styles are also included with corresponding Play Along tracks. Finally, there are numerous percussion ensembles in the book, as well as several extended World Percussion Play Along tracks to be performed with written and improvised percussion parts. Enjoy!

Foreword

Teaching percussion at the beginning level always has presented many challenges with most college methods classes allowing little time for development of percussion performance skills. Areas usually covered include snare drum (grips and rudiments) and perhaps some limited mallet, timpani or auxiliary information. Some oft-neglected but important topics include:

- Drumset
- Improvisation (rhythmic and melodic)
- World Percussion
- Concert Accessories
- Literature (solos, ensembles)
- Methods and Pedagogy (videos and play-alongs)
- Listening
- Marching Percussion

Snare drum technique, keyboard mallet technique, timpani fundamentals and basic concert percussion skills must be covered to form a solid foundation for extended and long-term growth. However, introducing new concepts and ideas, along with utilization of new information technology – CDs, videos, computers and play-alongs – can elevate the beginner to a whole new musical level faster and more effectively. These new focus areas reflect current trends, fresh techniques, varied student interests, new technologies and numerous styles inherent in today's music, including world music and improvisation, both of which are included in the National Standards for Music Education.

Drumset
Nearly every beginning percussionist wants to play drumset, and many start banging right away on sets they coerced their parents into purchasing. Opportunities for drumset performance in traditional percussion education are very limited and usually don't become available until late middle school or high school, when students perform in jazz band or combos. However, the drumset should be integrated into the percussion section as soon as possible, depending entirely on instruments, personnel and literature available, and should reflect the diversity of style utilized in the band program.

Improvisation
As suggested in the National Standards, improvisation (rhythmic and melodic) plays an important role in a student's musical development. It makes sense to start this process immediately on all percussion instruments, including mallet keyboards. The act of improvising in a musical fashion provides many benefits to the player:

- Stronger sense of time
- Improved sense of phrasing
- More developed rhythmic awareness
- Stronger melodic sense
- Clearer sense of form

World Percussion
In many K-4 general music classes, the current focus is on multicultural or world music, which utilizes creative movement, improvisation and group performance (hand drumming, drum circles). But as we progress to school band programs, many of those important learning concepts fall by the wayside. Granted, the concert band director must be concerned with many essential issues, but somehow, the sheer joy, spirit, energy, inventiveness, excitement, physical movement, and raw enthusiasm of those early years must find their way into the band room. Hand drumming can be integrated easily into contemporary band literature and percussion ensemble.

Stylistic Awareness

Attention to musical styles seems to arise in jazz band much more than in concert band, and that is due, in part, to the literature. The National Standards in Music Education identify the need for students to be versed in the music of other cultures, such as Brazilian, Cuban or African. Exposing students to a wide variety of musical styles in the very beginning can be very beneficial to existing general music curricula: Classical, Marches, Dixieland, Jazz, Rock, Funk, Pop, Rap, Country, Blues, Gospel, Brazilian, Afro-Cuban, African, Reggae, Klezmer, Mexican and Asian musical styles that students hear daily on CDs, in stores, on television, in video and computer games, in church or at the movies.

Percussion Ensembles

Percussion ensemble activity is perhaps the single most important way to both energize and unify the percussion section and to teach the section to play as a stand-alone musical ensemble. In my earlier years, it was always very special for us to get together and perform as a percussion ensemble; however, it seemed only to happen at contest time and not on a regular basis.

Duets/Trios/Multiple Percussion Solos

Offering different musical settings to the percussionists, such as solos, duets, and trios, builds performance awareness. The Percussive Arts Society (PAS) offers numerous lists of graded material.

Percussion Specialist

Many school music programs enjoy the luxury of having a "Percussion Specialist," a person hired solely to coach the concert percussion section, write for and work with the marching line, and teach private lessons. This proves to be a great asset to the band director, because the section can meet apart from the band and can learn at a more aggressive pace, covering material that can't be addressed in band rehearsal. Still, certain core materials, along with all of the newer concepts, must be present for the individual player and the section to develop and prosper in today's musical climate.

Suggestions for Using This Book

Congratulations on taking the initiative to learn more about the wonderful world of percussion! This book is written for college music majors with no percussion background, current music teachers who want to brush up on their percussion skills, methods professors, or anyone who is interested in expanding their percussion teaching and performance skills. Most of the exercises in the book are self-directed, but a percussion specialist could certainly help the learner acquire the techniques and ideas in this book.

Skills Summary

You'll find short *Skills Summary* sections in this book. The Skills Summary outlines the skills you will learn by the completion of a group of exercises.

Portfolio

Buy a three-ring binder to create your *Portfolio*. You'll probably keep this document throughout your teaching career. Your portfolio should be used to:

- Write your own weekly goals on what you choose to accomplish
- Complete Portfolio assignments suggested throughout this book
- Obtain copies of relevant percussion brochures (instruments, artists, etc.)
- Reflect on your own learning process

Skills Assessment

The *Skills Assessment* pages provide you with a way to form an educated opinion about your own progress. Most importantly, the rubic descriptors will teach you how to listen and improve your beginning percussion student's skills. Depending on your situation, use the Skills Assessment pages in any one of the following:

- *Self-Assessment* – Evaluate your own work before advancing to the next group of exercises.
- *Peer Assessment* – If you're a college student, practice evaluating each other's work.
- *Teacher Assessment* – If you're a percussion instructor, use the form to evaluate the work of your students.

Using points to evaluate progress is optional. Discovering how to improve your skills is far more important than circling a number from the rubic box. However, if you choose to assign points, use this guideline to help you determine when to start working on the next group of lessons:

EVALUATION GUIDELINE – Add up your points and proceed as suggested.

45 – 50 points Great! You're ready for the next group of lessons. Keep practicing rudiments with the CD every day to improve your skills.

34 – 44 points You're doing very well. The CD will help you refine your skills even more. You're ready for the next lesson, but spend an equal amount of time reviewing the group of exercises you just completed.

23 – 33 points Percussion fundamentals are vitally important. Take the time to practice those skills now. Then, repeat this evaluation, and when you've scored higher, move on to the next group of exercises with confidence.

0 – 22 points You've been too busy to practice. No more excuses now – just practice slowly, have fun and DO IT!

Learning Strategies

Here are four simple ideas to help you learn the skills presented in this book:

➤ **Sing every exercise before you play it.** Percussionists must have excellent aural skills to be successful. Begin each exercise by singing it on any neutral syllable, use numbers, or the singing and counting method of your choice.

➤ **Play with the CD's.** The exercise numbers in the book match the CD's track numbers. The professionally recorded discs will fine-tune your ears, expose you to diverse styles of music, and provide definitive aural modeling of how to play everything from snare drum rudiments to Brazilian samba rhythms.

➤ **Subdivide, subdivide, subdivide!** Percussionists must constantly subdivide to accurately play in the style and stay in the tempo of the music. Start subdividing rhythms in your head right away. This will solidify your own counting, and help your class play together.

➤ **Rotate parts.** There are many percussion ensembles in this book. Rotate parts so you'll have experience playing all of the instruments. More importantly, listen to the musical context of all percussion instruments. You'll note different volumes and stylistic nuances.

The National Standards for Music Education

This percussion course is correlated with many of the National Standards for Music Education to show current and future educators how to include multiple standards in music instruction. The following pages include a reference to which these nine National Standards for Music Education are included in each group of exercises:

1) Singing, alone and with others, a varied repertoire of music.
2) Performing on instruments, alone and with others, a varied repertoire of music.
3) Improvising melodies, variations, and accompaniments.
4) Composing and arranging music within specific guidelines.
5) Reading and notating music.
6) Listening to, analyzing, and describing music.
7) Evaluating music and music performances.
8) Understanding relationships between music, the other arts, and disciplines outside the arts.
9) Understanding music in relation to history and culture.

Play and Teach Percussion
Semester Synopsis and Timeline

EXERCISES	PAGES	INSTRUMENTS	RUDIMENT	SKILLS AND STYLES	CORRELATES WITH NATIONAL STANDARDS	TIMELINE* FOR SEMESTER COMPLETION
			SECTION 1			
1 - 15	8 - 12	Snare Drum	Single Stroke Roll / Multiple Bounce Roll / Double Stroke Roll	Identify and position snare drum, play matched grip	2, 5, 6, 7, 9	Weeks 1 - 2
16 - 18	13 - 17	Keyboard Percussion		Mallet grip, stroke, Reggae, Bluegrass	2, 3, 5, 6, 7, 9	Week 3
19 - 29	18 - 23	Triangle, Temple Blocks, Wood Block	Flam / Flam Tap	Concept of Time, Rhythm improvisation	2, 3, 5, 6, 7	Week 4
30 - 36	24 - 26	Snare Drum	Primary Strokes 5-Stroke Roll / 9-Stroke Roll	Keyboard percussion transcribing, improvisation, S.D. cross stick, and Dixieland	2, 5, 6, 7, 9	Week 5
37 - 44	27 - 33	Tambourine, Maracas, Claves, Hand Cymbals, Bass Drum		Multiple techniques on all instruments, and Beguine, composition	2, 3, 4, 5, 6, 7, 8, 9	Week 6
45 - 49	34 - 37	Sus. Cym., Vibraphone		Multiple Sus. Cym. techniques, Swing rhythms	2, 3, 5, 6, 7, 9	Week 7
50 - 53	38 - 41	Snare Drum	Flam Tap in 6/8 / Flam Accent in 6/8	Keyboard percussion transcribing, S.D. cross stick, and Dixieland	2, 6, 7, 9	Week 8
54 - 62	42 - 45	Snare Drum	Ruff or Drag / Paradiddle / Drag Paradiddle #2 / Single Ratamacue / Triple Ratamacue	Aural performance, composition, W. C. Handy	2, 3, 4, 5, 6, 7, 8, 9	Week 9

EXERCISES	PAGES	INSTRUMENTS	RUDIMENT	SKILLS AND STYLES	CORRELATES WITH NATIONAL STANDARDS	TIMELINE FOR SEMESTER COMPLETION
63 - 66	46 - 51	Castanets, Cowbell	7-Stroke Roll RRLLRRL Flam Paradiddle L R L R R Rudiment Review	Rock sound within concert band section, ii-V-I progression, Aural performance, composition, Rock music	2, 3, 4, 5, 6, 7, 8, 9	Week 10
69 - 71	52 - 59	Timpani		German and French grips, ranges, dampening, rolls, arrangement, Aural performance	2, 3, 4, 5, 6, 7, 8, 9	Weeks 11 - 12

———— **SECTION 2** ————

EXERCISES	PAGES	INSTRUMENTS	RUDIMENT	SKILLS AND STYLES	CORRELATES WITH NATIONAL STANDARDS	TIMELINE FOR SEMESTER COMPLETION
1 - 11	60 - 70	Drumset		Set-up, tuning, 2-way, 3-way and 4-way coordination, Jazz Swing	2, 3, 5, 6, 7, 8, 9	Week 13
12 - 22	71 - 77	Drumset		Rock Groove, Hard Rock, fills, brushes, Aural performance, $\frac{12}{8}$ R&B Groove	2, 3, 5, 6, 7	Week 14
23 - 28	78 - 79	Drumset		Latin groove, Aural performance	2, 3, 4, 5, 6, 7	Week 15
29 - 37	80 - 84 85 - 90 91 - 97	African: Dawuro, Gankogui, Shekere, Djembe, Djun-Djun, Caxixi Afro-Cuban: Guiro, Timbales, Congas, Bongos Brazilian: Surdo, Agogo Bells, Pandeiro, Tamborim, Ganza		Performance technique and rhythms for each culture, keyboard improvisation using minor Pentatonic and blues scales, arrangement, rhythmic improvisation	2, 3, 4, 5, 6, 7, 8, 9	Weeks 16 - 18

* This is an ideal (and slightly ambitious) timeline to cover this entire book in one semester. Your circumstances and scheduling may require adaptations. Strive to learn and master every CD exercise. This book will be a lifetime resource throughout your entire teaching career.

SECTION 1 · CD #1 CONCERT PERCUSSION

Snare Drum

Skills Summary • Exercises 1 – 15

At the conclusion of Exercises 1 – 15, you will be able to:

- Define rudiments
- Demonstrate proper matched grip on snare drum sticks
- Set up a snare drum and identify all parts
- Play a single stroke roll
- Play a multiple bounce (buzz or closed) roll
- Play a double stroke (open) roll
- Identify the sounds of single stroke rolls, multiple bounce rolls, double stroke rolls

THE SNARE DRUM

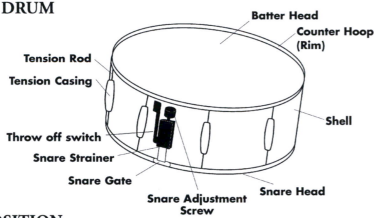

Batter Head
Counter Hoop (Rim)
Tension Rod
Tension Casing
Shell
Throw off switch
Snare Strainer
Snare Gate
Snare Head
Snare Adjustment Screw

PLAYING POSITION

A. Position the snare drum slightly below your waist.

B. Stand 6" to 8" away from the drum.

C. Position your upper arms and elbows comfortably to the side of your body. Avoid tension.

THE MATCHED GRIP

A. Extend your right hand as if shaking hands.

B. Place the stick between your thumb and first finger about 1/3 of the way up from the end of the stick. This is called the fulcrum point.

C. Curve your fingers around the stick.

D. Match the grip with your left hand.

E. Turn your hands over, palm down.

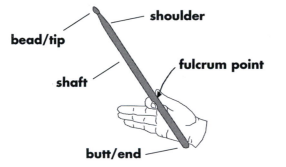

shoulder
bead/tip
fulcrum point
shaft
butt/end

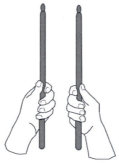

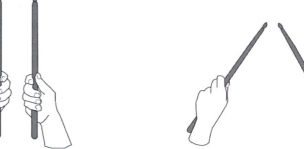

SNARE DRUM STROKE

A. Position the sticks in a "ready position" 1" to 2" over the head at an angle of about 60 degrees.

Note: To play on the rim of the snare drum, move far enough away from the drum to position the tips of the sticks just past the rim.

B. Use your wrist to raise the stick 6" to 8" above the head.

C. Drop the stick and allow it to rebound back to a position 6" to 8" above the head.

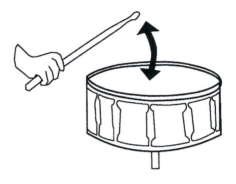

Note: Steps B and C should be one smooth and continuous motion.

D. Repeat steps B and C with the left hand.

NEW SKILL!

Rudiments

Rudiments are technical exercises which form the foundation for snare drum technique and reading skills. They are found in most concert band and orchestral music. The Percussive Arts Society (PAS) recognizes 40 different rudiments (see page 104). This book introduces 16 rudiments. All rudiments should be practiced slow–fast–slow as is demonstrated on CD#1.

⬤ **The exercise numbers in Section 1 match the CD#1 Track numbers.**

RUDIMENT

① SINGLE STROKE ROLL   ➤ **Practice slow-fast-slow.**

R L R L R L R L

The first rudiment is the single stroke roll. Listen to CD#1 Track 1 to hear how the single stroke roll should be practiced. When you practice R L R L (Right hand/Left hand) at various tempos, listen carefully to ensure you play steady strokes with even dynamics from both right and left hands.

② PLAY ALONG

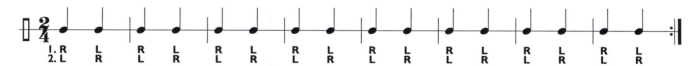

1. R L R L R L R L R L R L R L R L
2. L R L R L R L R L R L R L R L R

➤ **Name the three instruments who play on CD#1 Track 2:**_____

③ ACCOMPANY THE CD

1. R L R L R L R L R L R L R L R L R L R L R L R L R L R L R L R
2. L R L R L R L R L R L R L R L R L R L R L R L R L R L R L R L

➤ **Listen to how your written part enhances of CD#1 Track 3.**

4 SINGLE STROKE ROLL EXERCISE

Play 4 times.

5 ACCOMPANY THE CD

➤ **Name the melodic instrument featured on CD#1 Track 5:**_____

6 MULTIPLE BOUNCE (Closed) ROLL

Play a multiple bounce (closed) roll by learning to produce the maximum amount of "buzz" from each stroke. It is not necessary to count the number of bounces in each buzz stroke.

7 PLAY ALONG

8 ACCOMPANY THE CD

➤ **What instrument plays on the beat in CD#1 Track 8?**_____

9 ACCOMPANY THE CD

10 PLAY ALONG

Teaching Tip

As a music educator, you must constantly refine your own listening skills and develop listening skills in your students. Practice with the enclosed CD's often. When you're teaching, be sure to use a band method which offers CD recordings of examples and accompaniments. Practicing with professional musicians on a CD is more fun than practicing alone, and students are more likely to stay in band when they enjoy practicing!

11 BUZZ ROLL EXERCISES

RUDIMENT

12 DOUBLE STROKE (Open) ROLL $\sharp$ = $\sqcap\!\sqcap$
RRLL

At a slow tempo, strike the drum head with two strokes per hand (RRLL). As the tempo increases, let the stick rebound once and catch it to prevent it from rebounding again.

➤ **Practice slow-fast-slow.**

RR LL RR LL   RR LL RR LL

13 DOUBLE STROKE BASICS

➤ **Play accents after you can play all strokes evenly.**

R R L L   R R L L   R R L L   R R L L   R R L L   R R L L   R R L L   R R L L

➤ What sound is playing eighth notes on CD#1 Track 13?_____

14 ACCOMPANY THE CD

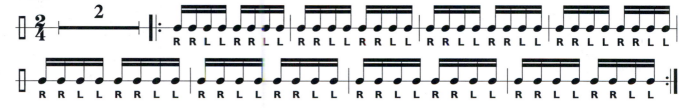

R R L L R R L L   R R L L R R L L   R R L L R R L L   R R L L R R L L

R R L L R R L L   R R L L R R L L   R R L L R R L L   R R L L R R L L

➤ What instrument plays the melody on CD#1 Track 14?_____

15 OPEN ROLL EXERCISE

Play 3 times.

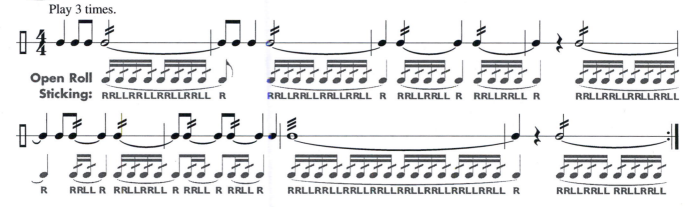

Open Roll Sticking: RRLLRRLLRRLLRRLL R   RRLLRRLLRRLLRRLL R   RRLLRRLL R   RRLLRRLL R   RRLLRRLLRRLLRRLL

R   RRLL R RRLLRRLL R RRLL R RRLL R   RRLLRRLLRRLLRRLLRRLLRRLLRRLL R   RRLLRRLL RRLLRRLL

Teaching Tip

Open rolls are used in most military and concert marches, drum corps, and marching band music. Use closed rolls in concert band, jazz, and orchestral music unless other instructions are specified.

Skills Assessment • Exercises 1 – 15

SKILLS: **This performance demonstrates:**

SKILLS:	10 9	8 7 6	5 4 3	2 1 0
Snare Drum Parts/Set-Up • Set-up and identify all parts of a snare drum.	Correct naming of all snare drum parts. Drum set-up is done efficiently, and is correctly set up slightly below the waist.	Incorrect or no names given to one or two snare drum parts. Drum set up is done correctly with verbal assistance.	Three or more parts of the snare drum are incorrectly identified. Drum is set up too high or too low for performance.	Insufficient preparation. Inability to properly set-up snare drum.
Single Stroke Roll • Play Ex. 1 and 5 in slow-fast-slow tempos.	Even single stroke rolls at slow-fast-slow tempos with equal dynamics in both hands. Posture, matched grip, stick height are consistent.	Some uneven rhythms in slow-fast-slow tempos and/or uneven dynamics between hands. Some tension and inconsistent stick heights.	Uncontrolled and uneven single stroke rolls in slow-fast-slow tempos most of the time. Uneven rhythms are due to inconsistent stick height.	Insufficient preparation on single stroke roll. Little evidence of slow-fast-slow practice.
Multiple Bounce (Closed) Roll • Play Ex. 6 and 11 in slow-fast-slow tempos.	Even, smooth beginning level multiple bounce rolls in slow-fast-slow tempos. Stick height is consistently even in both hands.	Some weakness in left hand's ability to sustain multiple bounces in slow-fast-slow tempos. Stick height is somewhat inconsistent.	Uncontrolled and uneven multiple bounce rolls due to inconsistent stick height in slow-fast-slow tempos.	Inability to create multiple bounces on drum head. Little evidence of slow-fast-slow practice.
Double Stroke (Open) Roll • Play Ex. 12 and 15 in slow-fast-slow tempos.	Even, beginning level double stroke roll in slow-fast-slow tempos. Stick height is correct all of the time.	Some problems sustaining double stroke rolls in slow-fast-slow tempos due to inconsistent stick height.	Difficulty in creating and sustaining double stroke rolls in slow-fast-slow tempos. Stick height is uneven.	Inability to create double stroke rolls. Little evidence of slow-fast-slow practice.
Listening Skills • Ask a percussion major or your instructor to play all three types of rolls without telling you which is being played. Identify and discuss.	Accuracy in identifying and discussing all three roll types. Eager and informed discussion participant.	Incorrect name given to one roll. Understands and discusses most characteristics correctly with encouragement from others.	Incorrect names given to two or more rolls. Several errors or limited discussion participation.	Inability to distinguish sounds of rolls, or did not participate in discussion.

PORTFOLIO – Percussion History

Briefly research the role and development of percussion instruments through the early military bands. Print your research and include in your portfolio.

Comments / Point Total:

Keyboard Mallet Percussion

Skills Summary • Exercises 16 – 18

At the conclusion of Exercises 16 – 18, you will be able to:

- Demonstrate proper keyboard mallet grip and stroke
- Identify and perform on a marimba
- Identify and perform on a xylophone
- Play by ear and notate a snare drum accompaniment on the rim
- Apply Sticking Principles for Keyboard Instruments
- Define style elements and artists of Reggae and Bluegrass music

PORTFOLIO – History

Briefly research percussion instruments invented and used from the 13th century to the late Renaissance era. Print your research in your portfolio.

Advance Your Skills

Practice simple keyboard percussion melodies using beginning band method books, piano methods, and other printed music resources. At the same time, improve your aural skills by practicing melodies by ear. Record progress in your portfolio.

RANGES FOR COMMON KEYBOARD PERCUSSION INSTRUMENTS

Chimes

Chimes sound where written.

Xylophone

Xylophones sound one octave higher than written, and are available in 2 1/2, 3, 3 1/2 and 4 octave models.

Marimba Ranges

Marimbas sound where written, and are available in 3 1/2, 4, 4 1/2 and 5 octave models.

Vibraphone

Vibraphones sound where written.

Orchestral Bells

Orchestra Bells sound two octaves higher than written.

KEYBOARD PERCUSSION – THE BELLS

KEYBOARD PERCUSSION PLAYING POSITION

A. Position the bells slightly below your waist and to the center of your body.

B. Position your upper arms and elbows comfortably to the side of your body.

C. Stand in a position that places the heads of the mallets over the center of the first row of tone bars. Avoid tension.

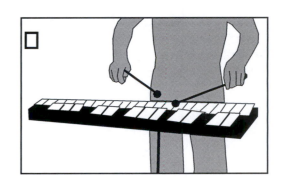

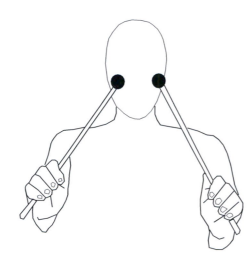

THE KEYBOARD MALLET GRIP

A. Grip each mallet between your thumb and the first joint of your first finger.

B. Wrap your fingers gently around each mallet without touching the mallet shaft.

THE KEYBOARD MALLET STROKE

A. Position the right hand stick in a "ready position" 2" to 3" over the keyboard.

B. Drop the mallet to the tone bar and bring it back immediately to the "ready position."

C. Repeat Steps A. and B. with the left hand.

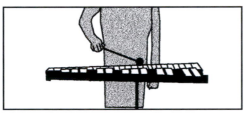

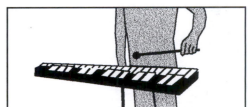

D. Alternate the right hand stroke and the left hand stroke. Bring the mallet back to the "ready position" after each stroke.

Note: The best tones are produced when the grip is relaxed and the mallet is in contact with the tone bar for as short a time as possible.

THE BELLS KEYBOARD

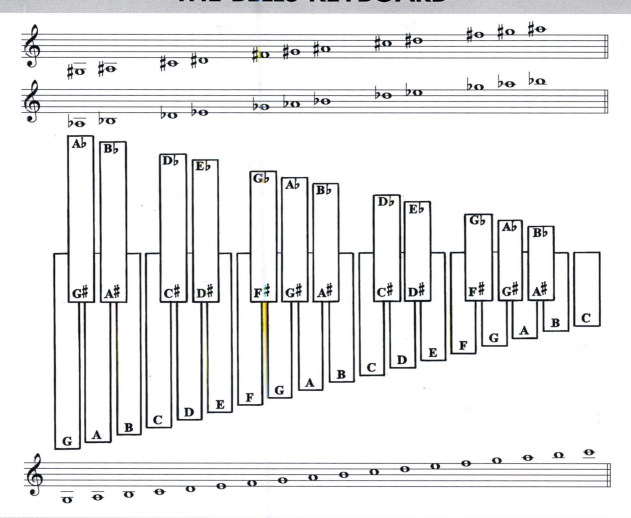

STICKING PRINCIPLES FOR KEYBOARD INSTRUMENTS

PRINCIPLE 1
Play large descending intervals right hand to left hand (R-L). See Example 1.

PRINCIPLE 2
Play large ascending intervals left hand to right hand (L-R). See Example 2.

PRINCIPLE 3
When there are two or more large descending intervals, stick right hand to left on the largest interval. See Example 3.

PRINCIPLE 4
When there are two or more large ascending intervals, stick left hand to right on the largest interval. See Example 4.

PRINCIPLE 5
When a large ascending interval and a large descending interval are separated by a repeated note or a smaller ascending or descending interval, set-up the large intervals when possible by double sticking the repeated note or smaller interval. See Examples 5 and 6.

PRINCIPLE 6
There are many ways to solve a given sticking problem. Experiment, improvise, and develop the ability to solve sticking problems independently and in a manner that is easiest and most comfortable for you.

Cobbler, Cobbler is performed on the MARIMBA. The marimba, originally from Africa, spread to the Americas and is used often in popular and concert music. It has hardwood or synthetic bars, with tubular resonators under each bar. The marimba is usually played with rubber or yarn mallets, and is capable of blending with almost any instrumental combination. Most high school solo marimba literature requires at least a 4-octave instrument. Advanced college level repertoire often uses a 5-octave marimba. Composers are regularly writing $4\frac{1}{3}$ to 5 octave marimba parts in current concert band and wind ensemble literature.

REGGAE – *A musical style mixing African and Caribbean rhythms often attributed to Jamaican sources.*

16 COBBLER, COBBLER

Rhythmically
(CD Intro)

Jamaican Street Song

➤ **Write in the sticking using the Keyboard Sticking Principles on page 15.**

➤ **Name the instrument playing the off-beats on CD#1 Track 16:** _____

17 COBBLER, COBBLER ACCOMPANIMENT BY EAR

NEW SKILL!

Listen to CD#1 Track 17. The rhythmic accompaniment is played on the rim of the snare drum using the following sticking:

STICKING: 1. R L RLRL R L R - L R LRLR L R L
2. R L RRLL R L R - L R LLRR L R L

Transcribe the snare drum rim rhythms on CD#1 Track 17. Write the rhythms below.

$\frac{2}{4}$ _____

Juba is performed on the XYLOPHONE. The xylophone, with origins in Southeast Asia and Africa, spread to the Americas and is a favorite percussion keyboard instrument of both composers and performers. It has real or synthetic rosewood bars, with tubular resonators under each bar. The xylophone is usually played with hard plastic or rubber mallets, which produce a pointed, brittle sound. The xylophone is one of the primary percussion instruments used in concert band, orchestra, and percussion ensemble literature.

BLUEGRASS – *A type of Anglo-American folk music originating around the mid-1940s in rural Appalachia.*

PERCUSSION ENSEMBLE

18 JUBA

Playfully

African-American Folk Song

➤ **Write in the sticking using the Keyboard Sticking Principles on page 15.**

➤ **What instrument adds fills on CD#1 Track 18?** _____

Skills Assessment • Exercises 16 – 18

SKILLS:	This performance demonstrates:			
Keyboard Percussion Posture and Mallet Grip • Apply to Ex. 16, 18.	**10 9** Relaxed, correct posture, mallet grip and ready position. Strokes are full with correct lift. Bars are consistently struck in the center.	**8 7 6** Some tension in body posture or grip. Ready position is correct most of the time, but strike area is not always in center of bar, or is too high/too low.	**5 4 3** Raised, tense shoulders. Mallets are occasionally gripped too tightly resulting in less tone. Stick height is often uneven. Tone is not full due to striking bar over the node.	**2 1 0** Insufficient preparation. Does not demonstrate proper position or mallet grip. Stroke area is over node, or is too low/too high.
Marimba • Play Ex. 16.	**10 9** Correct notes and rhythms at all times.	**8 7 6** Most notes and rhythms are correct.	**5 4 3** Frequent re-starts to correct note or rhythm errors.	**2 1 0** Insufficient preparation on marimba.
Snare Drum on Rim by Ear • Listen and play Ex. 17. Write out rhythms you hear and play.	**10 9** Accuracy in hearing, playing and writing out rhythms.	**8 7 6** Missed rest or used incorrect sticking at first, but repeat was accurate. Most rhythms written out correctly.	**5 4 3** Frequent re-starts and errors in playing by ear. Several errors in notating 16th notes and rest.	**2 1 0** Inability to play rhythms by ear.
Sticking Principles • Apply to Ex. 16, 18.	**10 9** Accuracy in applying all six sticking principles to both examples.	**8 7 6** One or two awkward stickings which are inconsistent with sticking principles.	**5 4 3** More than three awkward written stickings which are inconsistent with sticking principles.	**2 1 0** Inability to apply sticking principles.
Xylophone • Play Ex. 18.	**10 9** Correct notes and rhythms at all times.	**8 7 6** Most notes and rhythms are correct.	**5 4 3** Frequent re-starts to correct note or rhythm errors.	**2 1 0** Insufficient preparation on xylophone.

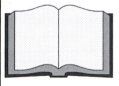

PORTFOLIO – Musical Styles and Sounds

• **Reggae** - Listen to at least two Reggae artists/albums. In your portfolio, write down at least three characteristics of Reggae music—instruments commonly used, unique rhythms, artists who helped define this style, and/or influences from other countries.

• **Bluegrass** - Listen to at least two Bluegrass artists/albums. In your portfolio, write down at least three characteristics of Bluegrass music—instruments commonly used, unique rhythms, artists who helped define this style, and/or influences from other countries, etc.

• **Timbre** - Describe the different timbres of a marimba and a xylophone. Include a list of three compositions/recordings featuring the marimba, and three compositions/recordings featuring the xylophone.

Comments / Point Total:

Flam, Flam Tap, Triangle, Temple Blocks, Woodblock

Skills Summary • Exercises 19 – 29

At the conclusion of Exercises 19 – 29, you will be able to:

- Play a Flam and a Flam Tap
- Identify and perform on Temple Blocks
- Identify and perform on a Wood Block
- Identify and perform on a Triangle
- Discuss the concept of "time" starting with fundamental beats
- Play a percussion ensemble

RUDIMENT

19 FLAM

L R L R L R L R   L R L R L R L R

➤ **Practice slow-fast-slow.**

The flam stroke is frequently used in snare drum performance. Composers and arrangers use the flam stroke to lengthen and strengthen notes.

To perform the RIGHT HAND (ʟR) FLAM stroke:

A. Position the left stick about one inch over the head and the right stick about six inches over the head in the "ready position."

B. Drop both sticks to the head. The left stick should strike the head slightly before the right stick. The result is a sound much like the word "FLAM."

C. Return both sticks to the "ready position" after the flam stroke.

 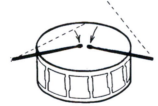 

READY POSITION   **STROKE**   **REBOUND POSITION**   **STROKE f-LAM**

To perform the LEFT HAND (ʀL) FLAM stroke:

A. Position the right stick about one inch over the head and the left stick about six inches over the head in the "ready position."

B. Drop both sticks to the head.

C. Return both sticks to the "ready position."

 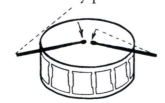 

READY POSITION   **STROKE**   **REBOUND POSITION**   **STROKE f-LAM**

20 ACCOMPANY THE CD

(CD Intro)

1. L R L R   L R L R
2. R L R L   R L R L   *sim.*

21 ALTERNATING FLAMS

Play 4 times.

L R R L L R R L L R R L L R R L L R R L L R R L L R R L L R R L L R

RUDIMENT

22 FLAM TAP

1. L R R   R L L
2. R L L   L R R

➤ **Practice slow-fast-slow.**

23 ACCOMPANY THE CD

➤ **What is the title of this song?**_____
Play the melody by ear on any keyboard mallet instrument.

(CD Intro)

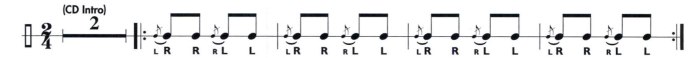

L R R R L L   L R R R L L   L R R R L L   L R R R L L

➤ **Name one instrument featured on the off-beats of CD#1 Track 23:**_____

Time

The concept of playing or singing in time must be taught to all musicians. For young musicians, playing or singing in time means, "Don't rush," or "Don't drag." In this sense, time is driven by pulse. The conductor sets the tempo, and that's exactly what should be played or sung so groups of musicians can perform together.

However, as musicians develop, playing with a good sense of time takes on a whole new meaning. This is especially important when performing or recording contemporary jazz, pop/rock, or Latin styles. Experienced musicians deliberately play behind, ahead, or dead-on the beat, depending on the requirements of the style of music.

Finally, time is connected to the concept of "Feel." One must play or sing with a good rhythmic sense, strong awareness of style subtleties, and the correct time feel (interpretation) for the style of music. At this level, time becomes a much broader concept than "staying with the stick." Musicians with an excellent sense of time excel because they are acutely aware of style differences and constantly listen and respond to what is happening in their ensemble.

The author often says, "Play with the time, don't play the time... let it happen!" Enjoy developing your own sense of time by first listening and analyzing jazz, Latin, pop/rock, classical, march, and world music CDs.

TRIANGLE

The triangle is an ancient musical instrument capable of producing many interesting sounds. The sound produced depends upon the size and weight of the triangle, the size and weight of the beater, the spot struck, and the type of stroke used. The triangle is one of the most frequently used instruments in concert band and orchestra literature. Triangle sizes range from 4 inches to 10 inches.

The triangle is suspended on a clip made of wood or metal. A thin cord (usually nylon fishing line) is strung through the holes on a clip. The clip can be found in most hardware stores. It's advisable to string a second nylon line in case the first one breaks.

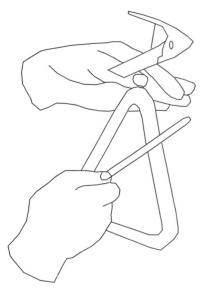

TO PLAY THE TRIANGLE:

A. Hold the instrument by its clip at chest level.

B. Grasp the triangle beater lightly near its end.

C. Strike the triangle opposite the open end about 1/3 of the way down from the top corner.

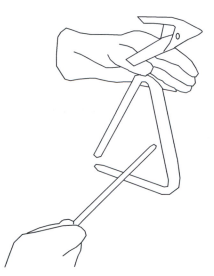

D. For a different effect, strike the lower bar. A softer dynamic level is produced by playing at the tip of the beater; a louder dynamic level is produced by playing at the center of the beater.

E. For rolls, move the beater rapidly back and forth in one of the closed corners.

TO STOP THE VIBRATION OF THE TRIANGLE:

F. To stop the vibration of the triangle, touch it gently with your fingers.

24 **TRIANGLE ETUDE**   *l.v. = let vibrate (do not dampen)*

25 **TRIANGLE ROLL**

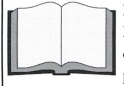

PORTFOLIO – Triangles
Practice rolls on various sizes of triangles. Note the pitch and ring differences. Listen to concert band, orchestra, and concert march music for different triangle effects. Write your observations in your portfolio.

TEMPLE BLOCKS

The temple blocks originated in China. They are usually played with medium or hard rubber mallets, and occasionally with drum sticks. Temple blocks are available in sets of 5 to 9 blocks, and are always arranged in keyboard style.

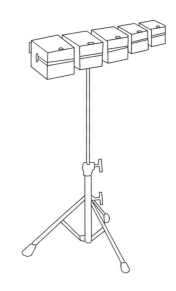

TO PLAY THE TEMPLE BLOCKS:

A. Strike each temple block in the center of the block over the resonating slit. Experiment to determine the best sound.

26 TEMPLE BLOCKS ETUDE

R L R L R L   R L L R   R L R R L R   L   R L R L R L   R L R L R L   R L R L R   L

WOODBLOCK

The woodblock originated in ancient China. Its sharp, woody sound is frequently used to create musical accents and to provide contrast to the percussive sound of drums or to the metallic sound of cymbals, triangle, or bells. The woodblock is played primarily with plastic, rubber, or wooden mallets, and occasionally with the tip or butt end of a drum stick.

TO PLAY THE WOODBLOCK:

A. Grip the woodblock at the far end of the block. Hold the woodblock at chest level to project the sound.

B. Strike the approximate center of the woodblock with a medium-hard rubber mallet or drum stick.

Note: Experiment to find the spot that produces the best sound. It is sometimes called the "sweet spot."

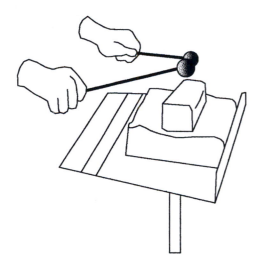

C. To perform rapid passages, set the woodblock on a firm, cushioned surface and strike with alternating strokes of mallets or drum sticks.

27 WOODBLOCK ETUDE

Play with hard rubber mallets.

➤ **Experiment with different mallet hardnesses.**

28 WOODBLOCK ETUDE

Play with snare drum sticks.

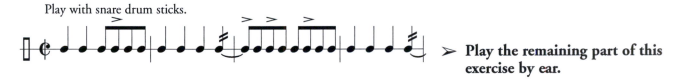

➤ **Play the remaining part of this exercise by ear.**

PORTFOLIO – Woodblock

Describe the differences in sound when a woodblock is played with a hard mallet and snare drum sticks. What sounds or images does a woodblock convey?

PERCUSSION ENSEMBLE

29 CLOCKS ROUND QUARTET

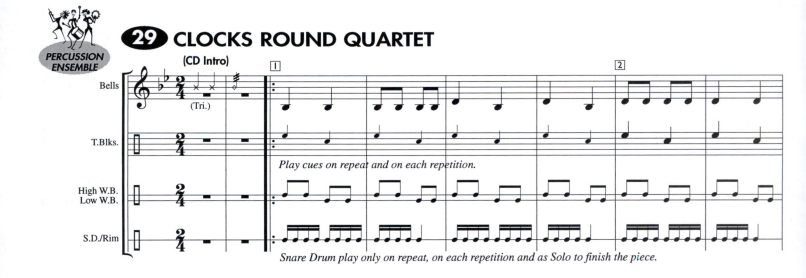

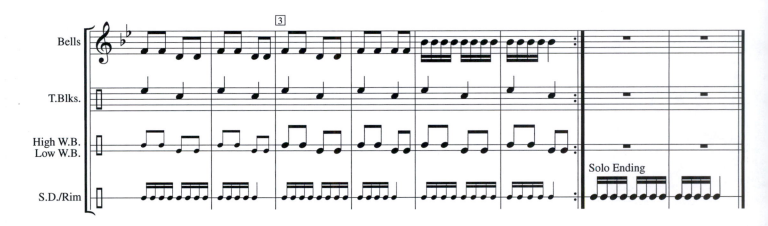

➤ **Play as a round. Be sure to rotate players on all parts. Improvise accompaniment rhythms on temple blocks, woodblock, and triangle.**

Skills Assessment • Exercises 19 – 29

SKILLS: **This performance demonstrates:**

SKILLS	10 9	8 7 6	5 4 3	2 1 0
Flam • Play Ex. 20, 21.	Consistently correct stick height resulting in properly executed flams.	Slightly too much space between grace note/primary note, or grade note is too loud due to inconsistent stick height.	Incorrect stick heights most of the time. Grace note starts too high, and/or primary note starts too low.	Insufficient flam preparation, or lacks understanding of how to play a flam.
Flam Tap • Play Ex. 23.	Consistently correct stick height resulting in properly executed flam taps.	Slightly too much space between grace note/primary note, or grace note is too loud due to inconsistent stick height.	Incorrect stick heights most of the time which cause soft taps, uneven tempo, and unbalanced rudiment.	Insufficient flam tap preparation, or lacks understanding of how to play a flam tap.
Auxiliary Instruments (Temple Blocks, Woodblock, Triangle) • Play Ex. 24, 26, 27, 28.	Consistently correct mallet choices and striking positions.	Minor problems in mallet choices and/or knowing how/where to strike each instrument.	Frequent incorrect mallet choices, and lacks thorough understanding of how/where to strike each instrument.	Insufficient preparation on mallet choices and knowing how/where to strike each instrument.
Aural Skills • Play Ex. 23 on keyboard percussion instrument by ear.	Accuracy in hearing and playing correct notes, intervals, and rhythm.	Missed two or three intervals or rhythms, but repeat was mostly accurate.	Frequent re-starts. More than four errors in playing by ear. Several incorrect intervals and/or rhythms.	Inability to play rhythms by ear, and/or serious difficulty in hearing intervals correctly.
Percussion Ensemble Balance • Play Ex. 29 with and without CD.	Attentive listening skills with sensitivity given to balance and style elements.	Minor errors during parts of round.	Difficulty in counting and playing round parts.	Inability to count and accurately play written parts in a round.

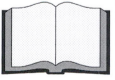

PORTFOLIO: CLASS ACTIVITY – The Concept of Fundamental Beats

To understand the concept of time, let's begin by discovering what beats are most important, or fundamental, in various styles of music. While listening to CDs of contemporary jazz, Afro-Cuban, Brazilian, rock, and traditional concert marches, snap your fingers, clap your hands, or stomp your feet to feel where the fundamental beats are in these styles. Then, discuss the following with your classmates:

1) What are the fundamental beats in swing music?_____

2) What are the fundamental beats in rock music?_____

3) What are the fundamental beats in traditional concert marches?_____

4) What beat does Afro-Cuban music center around?_____

5) What beat does Brazilian music center around?_____

Comments / Point Total:

Primary Strokes, Five- and Nine-Stroke Rolls

Skills Summary • Exercises 30 – 36

At the conclusion of Exercises 30 – 36, you will be able to:

- Understand and identify primary strokes
- Play a nine-stroke open roll
- Play a five-stroke open roll
- Demonstrate snare drum cross stick
- Perform keyboard percussion rolls
- Play keyboard percussion melodies by ear
- Improvise an accompaniment on woodblock

NEW IDEA!

PRIMARY STROKES

Primary stroke concept is the basis for playing double bounce rolls. The five-stroke roll is the most basic "numbered" roll. It consists of five distinct sounds, but is played using only 3 primary strokes. The first two create double bounces, and the third is just a single bounce.

RUDIMENT

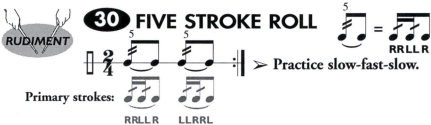

30 FIVE STROKE ROLL

➤ Practice slow-fast-slow.

Primary strokes:

RRLL R   LLRR L

31 FIVE STROKE ROLL EXERCISE

Play 4 times.

32 PLAY ALONG

(CD Intro)

Snares off

RUDIMENT

33 NINE STROKE ROLL

Primary strokes:

RR LL RR LL R   LL RR LL RR L

➤ How many primary strokes are there in the nine-stroke roll?_____
➤ Practice slow-fast-slow.

34 ACCOMPANY THE CD

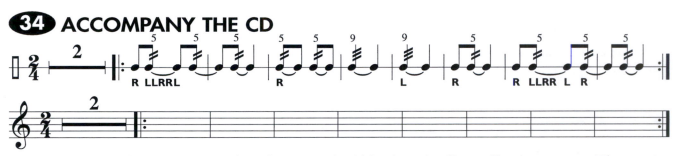

R LLRRL   R   L   R   R LLRR L R

➤ Play this melody on CD#1 Track 34 by ear, and add keyboard rolls to all quarter notes. Then, write it out on the staff.
➤ What instrument plays the off-beats on CD#1 Track 34?_____

Teaching Tip

Professional music organizations offer multiple resources, professional growth opportunities, networking, inspiring ideas, valuable connections and much more. If you're in college, be active in your CMENC chapter. If you're teaching, be sure to join MENC: The National Association for Music Education. Use the Internet to learn about IAJE (International Association of Jazz Education), PAS (Percussive Arts Society) and other professional music organizations. Be involved and stay connected!

SNARE DRUM CROSS STICK

The snare drum cross stick is a percussion effect that originated with the drum set. It is often used to play the clave rhythm in Latin music, and the back beat in swing music.

TO PLAY THE CROSS STICK:

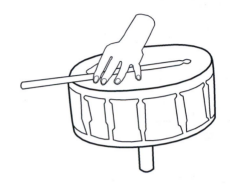

A. Position the drum stick with the tip of the stick resting against the head and the butt end of the stick across the rim.

B. Lift the butt end of the stick with the tip of the stick on the drum head, and strike it against the rim to produce the effect.

35 SNARE DRUM CROSS STICK

➤ Make sure you hit the rim with the same part of the stick each time to produce a consistent sound.

36 OH WHEN THE SAINTS GO MARCHING IN

PERCUSSION ENSEMBLE

➤ There are two versions (starts) on CD#1 Track 36. Practice with both starts.

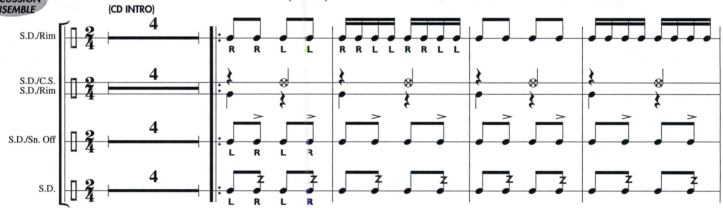

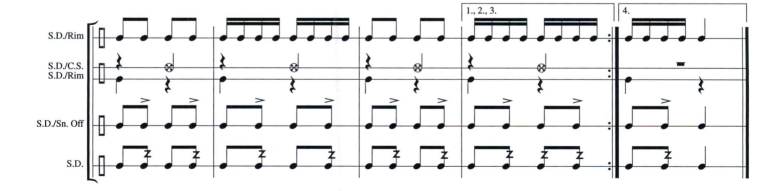

➤ Name three instruments featured on CD#1 Track 36 which are traditionally used in Dixieland music:_____
➤ Play the melody on xylophone and marimba by ear. Add rolls to all half notes.
➤ Improvise an accompaniment using woodblock.

Skills Assessment • Exercises 30 – 36

SKILLS: **This performance demonstrates:**

SKILLS:	10 9	8 7 6	5 4 3	2 1 0
Five-Stroke Roll • Play Ex. 30, 31 demonstrating primary stroke concept.	Smooth and precise five-stroke rolls. Correctly demonstrates and understands primary stroke concept.	Slightly inconsistent stick heights on primary strokes resulting in slightly uneven five-stroke rolls.	Inaccurate five-stroke rolls caused by incorrect number of bounces on primary strokes.	An inability to create five-stroke rolls. Lacks understanding of primary stroke concept.
Nine-Stroke Roll • Play Ex. 33, 34 demonstrating primary stroke concept.	Smooth and precise nine-stroke rolls. Correctly demonstrates and understands primary stroke concept.	Slightly inconsistent primary stroke stick height resulting in slightly uneven nine-stroke rolls.	Inaccurate nine-stroke rolls caused by incorrect number of bounces on primary strokes.	An inability to create nine-stroke rolls. Lacks understanding of primary stroke concept.
Snare Drum Cross Stick • Play Ex. 35.	Even, smooth, and precise cross stick. Consistently strikes rim with same part of the stick.	A few different cross stick sounds due to stick movement on the rim.	Incorrect stick position on drum, or stick often moves around resulting in irregular sounds.	A lack of understanding of S.D. cross stick technique.
Aural Skills • Play Ex. 34, 36 by ear.	Accurate melodic intervals and rhythms on both melodies.	Some interval errors on melodies, but rhythms are correct.	Frequent errors in both melodies and rhythms.	Inability to play melodies by ear.
Improvisation Skills • Improvise woodblock accompaniment on Ex. 36.	A rhythmic improvisation in time, in the style, and complements the written parts.	A rhythmic improvisation with minor lapses in time and/or style concepts.	A rhythmic improvisation without time and/or style concepts.	Inability to perform a rhythmic improvisation.

PORTFOLIO – Dixieland

Name three artists who helped define Dixieland music. What roles do instruments used in Dixieland music play – melodies, fills, on what beats, etc.? What instrumental techniques do you often hear in Dixieland music? What percussion rhythms and techniques do you often hear in Dixieland music? Print your research in your portfolio.

Comments / Point Total:

Tambourine, Maracas, Claves, Hand Cymbals, Bass Drum

Skills Summary • Exercises 37 – 44

At the conclusion of Exercises 37 – 44, you will be able to:

- Identify and play a tambourine (knuckles, fingertips, roll)
- Identify and play maracas
- Identify and play claves
- Compose an accompaniment using claves, maracas, and tambourine
- Identify and play hand cymbals (crash, choke)
- Identify and play a bass drum
- Play claves by ear and notate the rhythms

TAMBOURINE

Tambourine-like instruments have been depicted historically in many cultures throughout the world. The modern tambourine has changed little since Medieval and Renaissance times. The tambourine is used to perform a variety of strokes and rolls; it may be played with either hand. The tambourine is commonly used in orchestra, concert band, and rock 'n' roll music.

TO PLAY THE TAMBOURINE:

A. Hold the tambourine in one hand with the thumb positioned on the head (if it has a mounted skin head) or on the rim (if it has no head).

B. Wrap your fingers securely around the shell.

C. Strike the head or the rim with the knuckles of your other hand with a snap of the wrist. Pull your knuckles off the head or rim immediately.

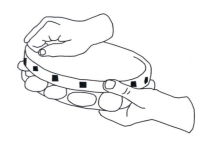

37 TAMBOURINE ETUDE

Play with your knuckles.

➤ Name a classical piece of music in which the tambourine is played with the knuckles:_____

D. For a lighter sound, strike the head or rim with the fingertips. Pull your fingertips off the head or rim immediately.

38 TAMBOURINE ETUDE

Play with your fingertips.

➤ Name a classical piece of music in which the tambourine is played with the fingertips:_____

E. To perform a roll, rotate the wrist rapidly back and forth. Most rolls are started with a tap of the fingers on the head or rim of the tambourine.

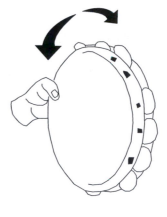

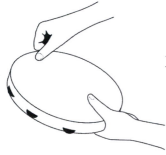

F. To perform a thumb roll – Moisten the thumb, and slowly move your thumb along the outer edge of the tambourine. This will take much practice.

G. For fast or loud passages – Use your wrist and arm to strike the tambourine on your knee with a downstroke. Use the knuckles of your opposite hand for the upstroke, as shown.

39 TAMBOURINE ROLL ETUDE

➤ **Name a rock 'n' roll piece of music in which a tambourine roll is played:**_____

THE MARACAS

Rattle-type instruments can be found in many forms in almost every culture dating to antiquity. Modern maracas are closely derived from Native North American rattles and have become an essential element of Latin American popular music. They are almost always played in pairs.

TO PLAY THE MARACAS:

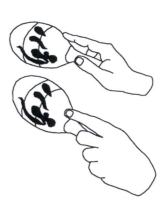

A. Hold the maracas at chest level and sharply flick your wrist downward.

40 MARACAS ETUDE

➤ **Maracas are often played in many Latin styles of music. Listen to recordings of mariachi bands and salsa style music, and hear how clearly the maracas rhythms are played. Name three other instruments usually played in mariachi bands:**_____

CLAVES

The claves consist of a pair of solid, hardwood cylinders that are struck together to produce a unique, penetrating sound. The Spanish word "clave" means "key," and the clave rhythm is "key" to all authentic African and Latin rhythms.

TO PLAY THE CLAVES:

A. Hold one clave lightly (against the fingernails) in a cupped hand.

B. Hold the other clave near one end with the thumb and first two fingers of the other hand.

C. Strike the clave in the cupped hand with the clave in the other hand. Experiment to determine the best sound.

41 CLAVES ETUDE

➤ **Listen to the tone of the claves on CD Track #41. Duplicate this sound.**

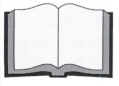

PORTFOLIO – Composition

Compose an 8-bar accompaniment using claves, maracas, and tambourine. Then, improvise additional rhythms on these instruments. Keyboard percussion instruments can be added playing any melody. In your portfolio, note how the improvised and composed accompaniments change the feel of the melodies.

Name three styles of Latin music:_____

HAND CYMBALS

The hand cymbals can create a brilliant and exciting musical effect. They have a rich history dating at least to the time of the Roman Empire. The hand cymbals are made in a wide variety of sizes and sound designs. The hand cymbals demand considerable physical strength and a high degree of musical sensitivity.

TO PLAY THE HAND CYMBALS:

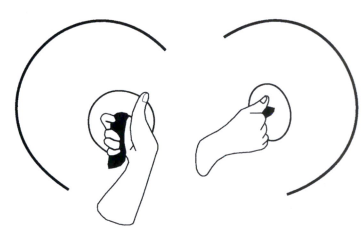

A. Stand with your feet apart and body weight evenly distributed over both feet.

B. Grasp each cymbal strap between the thumb and fingers, with the side of each index finger pressing firmly against each cymbal bell for support and control. For orchestral playing, the hands are not inserted through the straps.

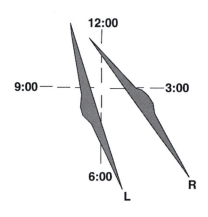

C. Hold the cymbals about 6" apart. The left cymbal should be in the 11 o' clock/5 o' clock position. The cymbals should be played at about chest level.

D. For a pleasant, full-sounding crash, move the right cymbal across and into contact with the stationary left cymbal.

E. After the "crash," move the cymbals apart.

42 HAND CYMBALS CRASH

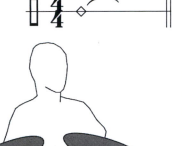

Listen how quickly the cymbal crash sound opens up (response time), the overtone spread, and the amount of decay. Cymbal sounds vary greatly. Fine tune your ears to the many sounds of these wonderful instruments.

TO STOP THE VIBRATION OF THE HAND CYMBALS:

F. Pull the edge of each vibrating cymbal firmly into the chest.

THE HAND CYMBAL CHOKE - To simulate the sound of the hi-hat (a component of the drumset):

A. Place the edges of the hand cymbals together against the chest and parallel to the ground.

B. Open and close the top cumbal to create the dry "chuck" sound of the hi-hat.

BASS DRUM

The bass drum evolved from its earliest forms as a long, cylindrical orchestral drum and a large-diameter military drum. It is played with a large paddled mallet (one for single notes and two for rolls).

PRELIMINARY PROCEDURE:

Stand behind the drum so that you can see the instrument, the music, and the conductor.

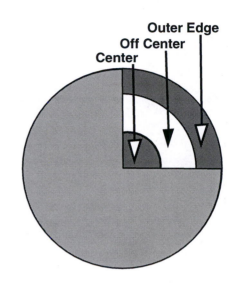

TO PLAY THE BASS DRUM:

A. Strike the batter head in the "Off Center" area with an up stroke that will draw sound from the head.

B. For a dryer sound (marches, rock beats), strike the batter head in the "Center" area with an up stroke.

C. For rolls, strike the batter head in the "Outer Edge" area with alternating strokes of a pair of mallets.

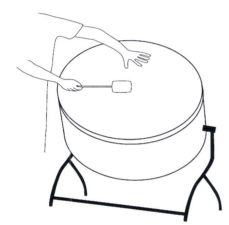

TO MUFFLE OR DAMPEN THE BASS DRUM:

A. Lay your hand on the batter head while striking the head.

B. Or, place your knee against the batter head while striking the head.

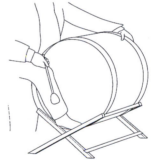

43 POLKA

PERCUSSION ENSEMBLE

➤ What instrument featured on CD#1 Track 43 is often used in polka bands?_____

PERCUSSION ENSEMBLE

44. PRACTICE EVERY DAY

➤ Play the claves by ear, then write it on the staff.

➤ Who is the composer of "Begin the Beguine?"_____

PORTFOLIO – Beguine (Music for dancing from Latin America)

Listen to 2-3 artists who play Beguine style music. What characteristic rhythms are used in this Latin style? What percussion instruments are used in Beguine music? Print your research in your portfolio. Be sure to include names of two artists who helped define Beguine style.

Label these instruments:

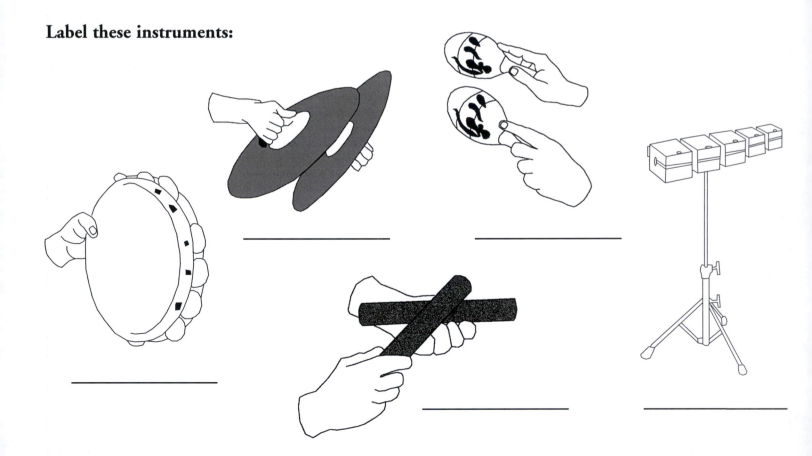

_____   _____   _____

_____   _____

Skills Assessment • Exercises 37 – 44

SKILLS: This performance demonstrates:

	10 9	8 7 6	5 4 3	2 1 0
Auxiliary Instruments (Tambourine, Maracas, Claves) • Play Ex. 37, 38, 39, 40, 41.	Consistently correct technique and tone on tambourine, maracas, claves. Rhythms are precise throughout.	Too tight or too loose hand positions creating slightly muffled tone and/or uncontrolled rhythms.	Incorrect hand positions create uncontrolled rhythms and uncharacteristic tones for these instruments.	Inability to play or hold tambourine, maracas, and/or claves correctly.
Composition • 8 bars using Tambourine, Maracas, Claves.	Distinct tension/release phrase(s), complementary rhythms, rests, and musical use. Writing is balanced for ensemble.	Phrase(s) which lack tension/release. Ensemble is compromised due to excessive or sparse use of rhythms and rests.	A complete composition, but one which lacks in ensemble unity. Phrase(s) are not obvious. Rests and rhythms are not effective.	Little or no sense of phrase or shape. Composition does not use all three instruments, or is less than 8 measures long.
Concert Instruments (Hand Cymbals, Bass Drum) • Play Ex. 42, 43.	Consistently correct technique on hand cymbal crash, choke, and bass drum.	Too tight or too loose hands, or incorrect body position creating slightly muffled tone or decay.	Incorrect hand or body positions ressult in uncharacteristic tone or decay.	Inability to play or hold hand cymbals or bass drum correctly.
Percussion Ensemble Balance • Play Ex. 43, 44 with and without the CD.	Attentive listening skills with sensitivity given to balance and style elements.	An understanding of balance and style elements but adjustments are not always correct or consistent.	Minimal ability and awareness of how/when to adjust balance and style elements.	Insufficient attention to listening skills, balance, and style elements.
Aural Skills • Play and notate Claves part by ear on Ex. 44.	Accurate rhythmic performance, technique, and notation of claves part.	Minor rhythmic errors by ear or on written claves part.	Several rhythmic and/or written notation errors on claves part.	Inability to hear or notate claves part.

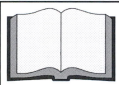

PORTFOLIO – Beguine

Listen to "Begin the Beguine" and "Beguine for Band." Name the percussion instruments used to create this style. In your portfolio, write down the percussion rhythms you hear which define Beguine style.

Comments / Point Total:

Suspended Cymbal, Jazz Beat, Vibraphone

Skills Summary • Exercises 45 – 49

At the conclusion of Exercises 45 – 49, you will be able to:

- Perform a suspended cymbal roll, jazz beat, and jazz beat with hand dampen
- Identify and perform on a vibraphone
- Discuss and demonstrate "jazz" concept of how to swing eighth notes
- Demonstrate and write out a suspended cymbal part by ear

THE SUSPENDED CYMBAL

The history of cymbals is one of the oldest and most interesting of all musical instruments, dating at least to the time of the Roman Empire. Modern cymbals are made in a wide variety of sizes and sound designs. The suspended cymbal is played with a variety of sticks, mallets, and beaters, each selected to produce a particular musical effect.

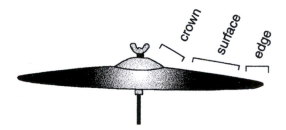

FOR A BRILLIANT CRASH SOUND:

A. Strike the edge of the cymbal with the shoulder of a drum stick. For a less brilliant sound, strike the surface of the cymbal near the edge with a yarn mallet or the tip of a drum stick.

TO PRODUCE A ROLL ON THE SUSPENDED CYMBAL:

B. Strike the surface of the cymbal near the edges with alternating and moderately slow strokes of a pair of soft to medium-soft yarn mallets. Play the roll with alternated, mostly slow strokes using height to vary the dynamics.

45 SUSPENDED CYMBAL ROLL

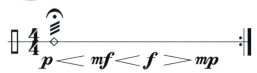

➤ **Listen carefully to the sound of the suspended symbal roll. Composers often use crescendo on a suspended cymbal roll to create excitement, anticipation, or dramatic effects. Match the gradual crescendo and decrescendo on CD#1 Track 45.**

FOR SPECIAL EFFECTS:

C. Strike the crown of the cymbal with a drum stick.

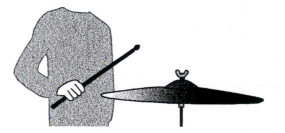

D. Draw a metal triangle beater quickly across the surface of the cymbal.

TO STOP THE VIBRATION OF THE SUSPENDED CYMBAL:

E. Grasp the edge of the vibrating cymbal between the fingers and thumb of one or both hands.

46 BUBBLE GUM

➤ What instrument plays a counter melody on CD#1 Track 46?_____

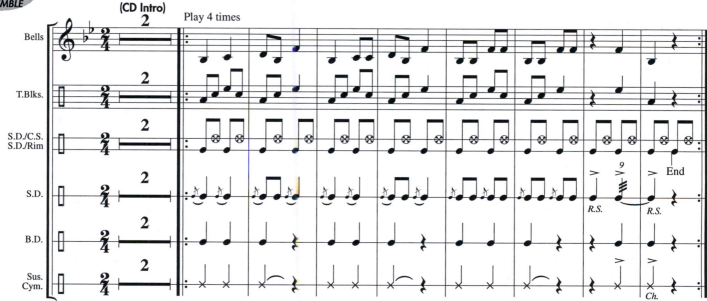

Teaching Tip*

When selecting cymbals for use in concert bands, orchestras, jazz ensembles, and marching bands, keep the following in mind. *Symmetrically hammered* cymbals offer a more balanced array of overtones with an emphasis toward the mid to upper-mid range of sound. *Randomly hammered* cymbals often produce more body of overtones with emphasis in the lower sonic range. *Heavier cymbals* will bring out ride cymbal patterns more clearly because the overtones are less apparent. Finally, *lighter cymbals* create a wider spread of overtones which sometimes interfere with stick articulation with ride cymbals, but will offer a quick response which is ideal for crash effects. For more information, consult cymbal manufacturers online, or talk with them at state, regional and national music conferences.

*Special thanks to John King, Director of Education at Avedis Zildjian Company.

47 SUSPENDED CYMBAL - JAZZ BEAT

Looks like:	Sounds like:

48 SUSPENDED CYMBAL - JAZZ BEAT WITH HAND DAMPEN

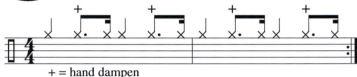

+ = hand dampen

➤ Exercises 47 and 48 are fundamental to playing drumset successfully. Duplicate the sound, style and tempos played on CD#1 Tracks 47 and 48.

Down By the Station (Jazz Swing Style) is performed on the VIBRAPHONE. The vibraphone, developed in the United States, is a popular jazz and orchestral music instrument. It has metal bars which produce a rich sustained tone unique to the instrument. Its characteristic vibrato is produced by electrically driven fans in tubular resonators just below the bars. The vibraphone is usually played with yarn or cord mallets. Most vibraphones have a range of three octaves.

49 DOWN BY THE STATION

To create the swing feel, play all eighth notes as ♪♪.

American School Song

➤ Play the suspended cymbal part using the jazz beat you learned in Exercise 47. Write those rhythms on the staff.

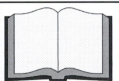

PORTFOLIO – Vibraphone Artists
Listen to and list the names of five different vibraphone artists in your portfolio. Describe the styles of music they play, and the ways composers use the vibraphone to create different effects in music.

Comments / Point Total:

Skills Assessment • Exercises 45 – 49

SKILLS: **This performance demonstrates:**

SKILLS:	10 9	8 7 6	5 4 3	2 1 0
Sus. Cym. Roll • Play Ex. 45 with and without the CD.	Smooth rolls with controlled dynamics due to correct stick height adjustments.	Even rolls, but dynamics lack control due to inconsistent stick height adjustment.	An inability to play dynamics due to stick height which is too high, and/or incorrect striking area.	Insufficient practice, and a lack of understanding of how/where to strike Sus. Cym.
Jazz Beats • Play Ex. 46, 47.	Accurate, precise time and rhythms. Hand dampen is released on time.	Slightly uneven or unsteady rhythms and time. Stick is too heavy. Hand dampen is often late.	Time is not steady or solid. Dotted rhythms are rushed or dragged. Left hand does not dampen or release on time.	A lack of practice and understanding of how to play jazz beats on suspended cymbal.
Vibraphone • Play Ex. 49.	Accurate striking area with correct swing rhythms on eighth notes.	Stick height and striking area vary compromising swing rhythms. Some inaccurate notes.	Minimal ability to play swing eighth notes, and/or often strikes bars on nodes.	Inability to play swing eighth notes. Stick height is inconsistent.
Percussion Ensemble Balance • Play Ex. 48 with and without the CD.	Attentive listening skills with sensitivity given to balance and style elements.	An understanding of balance but adjustments are not always correct.	Minimal ability and awareness of how/when to adjust balance and style elements.	Insufficient attention to listening skills, balance, and style elements.
Aural Skills • Play and notate Sus. Cym. part by ear on Ex. 49.	Accurate rhythmic performance, technique and notation of Sus. Cym. part.	Minor rhythmic errors on written Sus. Cym. part.	Several rhythmic and/or written notation errors on Sus. Cym. part.	Inability to hear or notate Sus. Cym. part.

PORTFOLIO – Jazz Styles

In your portfolio, listen to recordings and list the names of at least two different jazz artists for each of the following styles. Briefly describe the styles and unique characteristics, of the music they play:

• Dixieland –

• Swing –

• Be bop –

• Funk –

Comments / Point Total:

Flam Tap in 6/8, Flam Accent in 6/8

Skills Summary • Exercises 50 – 53

At the conclusion of Exercises 50 – 53, you will be able to:

- Identify and play a Flam Tap in 6/8 meter
- Identify and play a Flam Accent in 6/8 meter
- Play a simple melody in various keys by ear
- Create a school percussion budget for your portfolio

FLAM TAP IN 6/8

> **Practice slow-fast-slow.**

50 LITTLE TOM TINKER

FLAM ACCENT IN 6/8

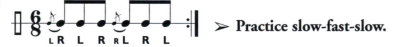

> **Practice slow-fast-slow.**

51 ACCOMPANY THE CD

Play 4 times.

> **Cover up the melody to "Little Tom Tinker" above, and play Exercise 51 on any keyboard mallet instrument by ear.**

52 ITSY BITSY SPIDER

Reggae style

United States

> What instrument plays melodic fills on CD#1 Track 52?_____

> In what style of music is this instrument traditionally used?_____

PORTFOLIO – Budget

Imagine it's September 21 in your first year of teaching, and your principal informs you your instrumental music budget for the next school year is due on October 15. Here's an exercise to help prepare you for the real world of teaching. This is an example of basic percussion instruments each school should provide for band and orchestra students. In your portfolio, create a scenario of percussion instruments your school currently owns and a percussion budget. For example, suppose you are teaching in a middle school with 500 total students and an instrumental music budget of $2500. What will you spend on new percussion instruments, new music, repairs, maintenance costs, awards, dues, fees, and miscellaneous expenses? Print your findings in your portfolio. Be sure to include manufacturers' brochures and price lists.

Basic Concert Percussion Instruments
Bass drum and stand
Snare drums and stands
Hand cymbals and stands
Suspended cymbal and stand
Orchestra bells
4 Pedal Timpani (32", 29", 26", 23")
Chimes and beaters
Xylophone(s)
Marimba(s)
Trap tables, stick trays
Concert Tom-toms
Tam-tam
Bongos

Accessories
Triangles and beaters
Claves
Woodblock
Temple Blocks
Sleigh bells
Castanets
Maracas
Cowbell
Whistles
Guiro
Ratchet
Finger cymbals

Jazz Oriented Instruments
Drumset
Vibraphone
Congas

Marching Percussion
(Depends on number of players)
Snare drums
Quad toms
Various sizes of tunable bass drums
Mallets and sticks
Keyboard instruments for outdoor use

Basic World Percussion Instruments
African Instruments: Dawuro, Gankogui, Shekere, Djembe, Djun-djun, Caxixi
Afro-Cuban Instruments: Guiro, Timbales, Congas
Brazilian Instruments: Surdo, Agogo Bells, Pandeiro, Tamborim, Ganza

Miscellaneous Needs: Heavy duty, adjustable music stands, instrument storage areas, print music storage areas, folders, marching folders, lyres, uniforms cleaning/repair, acoustic shells.

Yearly Budgets Must Also Include: New music costs, repair and maintenance costs, awards, dues, and fees.

53 BINGO
(CD Intro)

Gaily

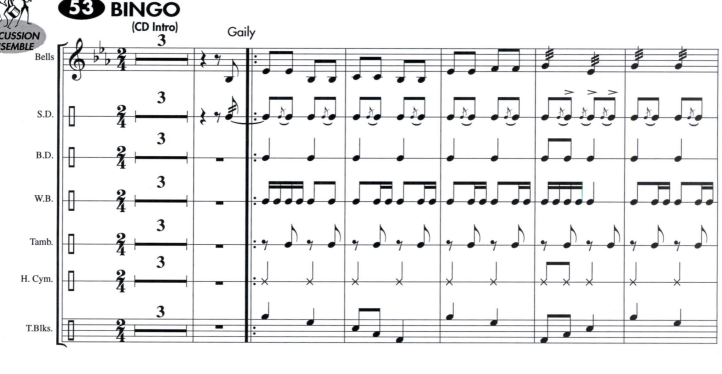

➤ Play the melody in various keys without using the CD.

➤ What instrument plays fills on the off-beats on CD#1 Track 53?_____
In what style of music is this instrument traditionally used?_____

Teaching Tip

After your students have developed solid facility using two mallets (scales, arpeggios, chromatic melodies, etc.), they should begin to learn four mallet technique. There are several different grips and techniques required to master four mallet technique, and each needs extensive explanation and specific technical exercises. Before your percussionists enter high school, encourage them to begin studying from one of these recommended mallet books so they can begin to explore the plentiful area of four mallet solo repertoire.

Method of Movement for Marimba	Leigh Howard Stevens (Marimba Productions)
Fundamental Method for Mallets	Mitchell Peters (Alfred)
Four-Mallet Studies for Marimba	Anthony Cirone (Warner Bros.)
Master Technique Builders for Vibraphone and Marimba	Anthony Cirone (Warner Bros.)
Four-Mallet Technical Studies	Garwood Whaley (JR Publications)

Skills Assessment • Exercises 50 – 53

SKILLS: This performance demonstrates:

	10 9	8 7 6	5 4 3	2 1 0
Flam Tap in $\frac{6}{8}$ • Play Ex. 50.	Properly executed flam taps in $\frac{6}{8}$ with consistently correct stick height.	Too much space between flam and tap, or tempo is slightly uneven.	Incorrect stick heights most of the time which cause soft flam taps, uneven tempo, and unbalanced rudiment.	Insufficient flam tap preparation, or lacks understanding of how to play a flam tap.
Flam Accent in $\frac{6}{8}$ • Play Ex. 51 on snare drum.	Properly executed flam accents in $\frac{6}{8}$ with consistently correct stick height.	Stick height is inconsistent resulting in too much/too little space between flam accent and tap.	Incorrect stick heights most of the time which cause soft flam accents, uneven tempo, and unbalanced rudiment.	Insufficient flam accent preparation, or lacks understanding of how to play a flam accent.
Aural Skills • Play Ex. 53 in two different keys chosen by you, your peers, or your instructor.	Accurate melodic intervals and rhythms on both melodies.	Two to four errors on melodies, but rhythms are correct.	Five to nine errors in both intervals and rhythms.	Inability to play melodies by ear.

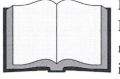

PORTFOLIO – Budget Five Year Plan

In your portfolio, create a five-year plan to obtain percussion instruments from your imaginary (or real) teaching situation. Write rationales describing why you feel the purchase of these additional instruments is necessary to benefit your students and your school music program. Share your findings with other classmates at the end of the semester.

Comments / Point Total:

Drag, Paradiddle, Drag Paradiddle #2, Single Ratamacue, Triple Ratamacue

Skills Summary • Exercises 54 – 62

At the conclusion of Exercises 54 – 62, you will be able to:

- Identify and play a Ruff (or Drag)
- Identify and play a Paradiddle
- Identify and play a Drag Paradiddle #2
- Identify and play a Single Ratamacue
- Identify and play a Triple Ratamacue
- Play a melody and improvise a duet part by ear
- Compose and perform 8-bar snare drum solo using at least five rudiments

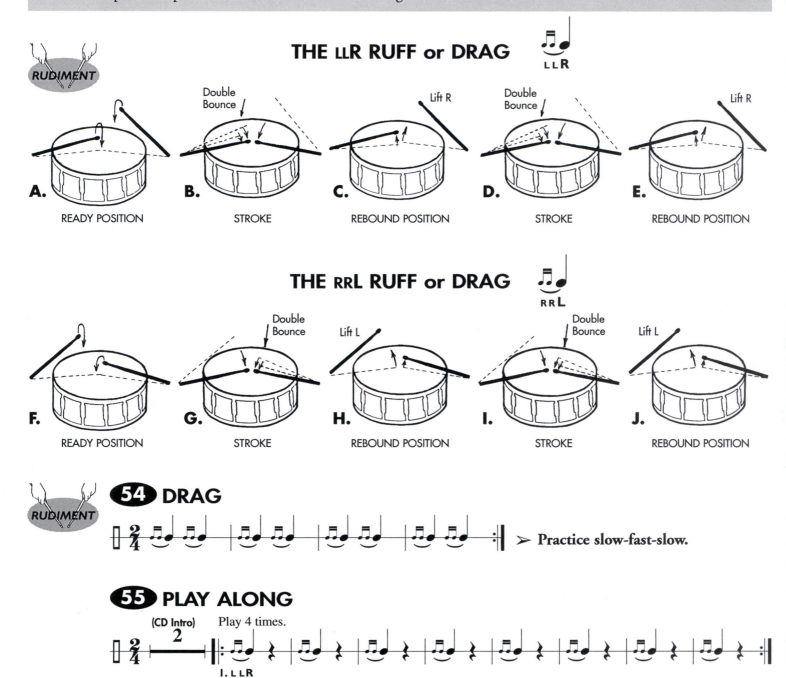

RUDIMENT

THE LLR RUFF or DRAG   LLR

A. READY POSITION B. STROKE C. REBOUND POSITION D. STROKE E. REBOUND POSITION

Double Bounce — Lift R — Double Bounce — Lift R

THE RRL RUFF or DRAG   RRL

F. READY POSITION G. STROKE H. REBOUND POSITION I. STROKE J. REBOUND POSITION

Double Bounce — Lift L — Double Bounce — Lift L

RUDIMENT

54 DRAG

2/4   > Practice slow-fast-slow.

55 PLAY ALONG

(CD Intro) 2   Play 4 times.

2/4

1. L L R
2. R R L
3., 4. Alternate sticking

56 ACCOMPANY THE CD

S.D.

57 ACCOMPANY THE CD

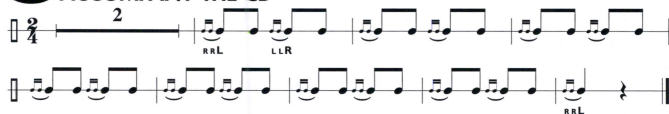

➤ Play the melody by ear on marimba and xylophone. Add rolls to all quarter notes and half notes.
➤ Improvise a duet part with the melody on any keyboard percussion instrument. Improvise rhythmic accompaniments using other percussion instruments.

58 THE PARADIDDLE

R L R R   L R L L

➤ Practice slow-fast-slow.

59 ACCOMPANY THE CD

Play 4 times.

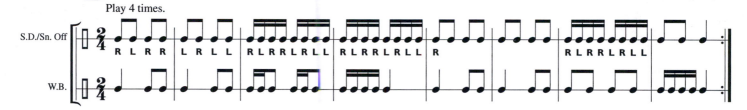

S.D./Sn. Off

R L R R   L R L L   R L R R L R L L   R L R R L R L L   R   R L R R L R L L

W.B.

DRAG PARADIDDLE #2

R LLR LLR L R R   L RRL RRL R L L

➤ Practice slow-fast-slow.

60 ACCOMPANY THE CD

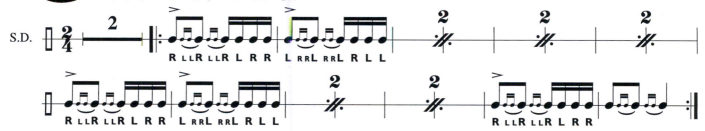

S.D.

R LLR LLR L R R   L RRL RRL R L L

R LLR LLR L R R   L RRL RRL R L L   R LLR LLR L R R

➤ Name two melodic instruments you hear on CD#1 Track 60:_____
➤ What style of music is featured on CD#1 Track 60?_____
    Give two examples to support your answer.

Rudiments Practice Hint

As you practice rudiments slow-fast-slow with and without the CD, strive to improve your endurance. Hold the fastest tempo longer. Increase your speed and flexibility without losing volume or power. Stay relaxed.

SINGLE RATAMACUE

➤ **Practice slow-fast-slow.**

61 PLAY ALONG

TRIPLE RATAMACUE

➤ **Practice slow-fast-slow.**

62 ST. JAMES INFIRMARY

W. C. Handy

➤ **Indicate which are single or triple ratamacues by writing "SR" or "TR" above the corresponding rudiment.**

PORTFOLIO – W. C. Handy and Composition

W. C. Handy is often called the Father of the Blues. Find out why, and discuss with your colleagues. Record your observations and research in your portfolio.

Compose an 8-bar snare drum solo using at least five of the rudiments you've learned, and include dynamics. Perform your solo for the class.

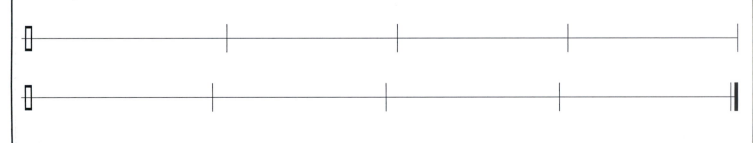

Skills Assessment • Exercises 54 – 62

SKILLS: **This performance demonstrates:**

SKILLS	10 9	8 7 6	5 4 3	2 1 0
Rudiments • Drag • Paradiddle	Both hands consistently strike with same power and velocity.	Some ruffs with double strokes which are too loud (sticks are too high), or primary notes which are too soft (sticks are too low). Paradiddle rhythms are slightly uneven.	Difficulty in maintaining fast tempos on paradiddles. Drags include many unbalanced/weak sounds due to incorrect stick heights.	Insufficient practice on ruffs and paradiddles.
Rudiments • Drag Paradiddle #2 • Single Ratamacue • Triple Ratamacue	Both hands consistently strike with same power and velocity.	Some uneven rudiments in fast tempos. Some double strokes are too loud (sticks are too high) or primary notes are too soft (sticks are too low).	Difficulty in maintaining fast tempos. Many rudiments are unbalanced or weak due to incorrect stick heights.	Insufficient practice on drag paradiddle #2, single ratamacue and triple ratamacue.
Snare Drum Composition • Use at least five rudiments in 8-bar solo.	Distinct tension/release phrase(s), complementary rhythms, rest, and musical use of at least five rudiments.	Three or four rudiments used in 8-bar composition. Phrases are not obvious.	One or two rudiments used in 8-bar composition with little sense of phrasing.	No rudiments used, or composition is less than 8 bars long.
Aural Skills • Play Ex. 57 on keyboard percussion by ear.	Accurate melodic intervals and rhythms on both melodies. Rolls are even and smooth.	Some interval errors on melody, but rhythms are correct. Some rolls are uneven due to inconsistent stick height.	Frequent errors in both intervals and rhythms. Rolls are uneven due to inconsistent stick height and lack of practice.	Inability to play melody by ear. Rolls are inaccurate due to incorrect stick height and lack of practice.
Improvisation • Improvise Keyboard Percussion duet on Ex. 57. • Improvise auxiliary percussion accompaniment on Ex. 57.	harmonic and rhythmic improvisations include effective tension/release phrases. Accompaniment style is characteristic throughout.	Tension/release in some phrases, but some intervals do not resolve to complement melody. Accompaniment style includes a few incorrect rhythms.	Harmonic and rhythmic improvisations lack in tension/release phrases. Accompaniment style is not clear due to misplaced uncharacteristic rhythms.	Inability to perform rhythmic or harmonic improvisations with a sense of composition, tension/release or characteristic rhythms.

PORTFOLIO – Beethoven

Examine Beethoven's use of percussion instruments in all nine symphonies. In your portfolio, note how Beethoven changed the use of percussion instruments for all other composers.

Comments / Point Total:

Castanets, Cowbell, Rock Drumset Sound, Seven-Stroke Roll, Flam Paradiddle, ii-V-I

Skills Summary • Exercises 63 – 68

At the conclusion of Exercises 63 – 68, you will be able to:

- Identify and perform on castanets
- Identify and perform on a cowbell
- Play a seven-stroke roll
- Play a flam paradiddle
- Create a rock drumset sound from the concert band percussion section section

- Improvise Latin and rock style accompaniments
- Practice major scales and arpeggios on keyboard percussion
- Practice the scales from the ii-V-I chord progression

THE CASTANETS

The castanets are descended from clappers, ancient instruments found in many cultures throughout world history. The castanets are widely used in Spanish music, especially to accompany dancing.

TO PLAY THE PADDLE CASTANETS:

A. Hold the paddles at chest level and quickly flick your wrist downward.

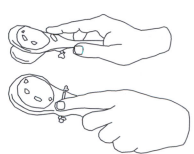

TO PLAY CASTANETS MOUNTED ON A STAND:

A. Tap the rhythms with your fingertips.

63 CASTANETS ➤ Be sure your rhythms are precise. Match the CD.

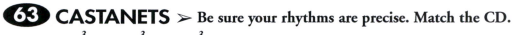

PORTFOLIO – Castanets

Write the titles of one classical piece and one pop music piece which use castanets in your portfolio.

How do flamenco dancers use castanets? Write your observations in your portfolio.

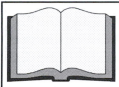

THE COWBELL

The cowbell, originally used to monitor the whereabouts of cattle, has found its way into many different musical styles and cultures. The cowbell is either hand-held or mounted; it is played primarily with a drumstick, and occasionally with an assortment of beaters, mallets, and sticks. The cowbell may be played with either hand.

TO PLAY THE COWBELL:

A. Hold the cowbell in the palm of your hand.

B. Strike the cowbell above its open end with the butt end of a drum stick. For a lighter sound, strike the center of the cowbell with the tip of a drum stick. Experiment to determine the best sound.

64 MUTED COWBELL

Play 4 times.

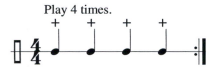

65 MEXICAN HAT DANCE

There are two versions (starts) of *Mexican Hat Dance* on CD#1 Track 65. Play the melody by ear on the second start. Try not to look at your music!

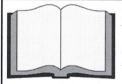

PORTFOLIO – What's Missing?

What percussion instrument could be added to "Mexican Hat Dance" which is usually heard in this style? Improvise an accompaniment using this instrument added to improvised accompaniments with snare drum, maracas, and castanets.

KEYBOARD PERCUSSION PRACTICE

Practice this pattern on all twelve major scales frequently. Transpose it up by half-steps, or use the Circle of Fifths to cover all twelve keys. Increase your speed without rushing the sixteenth notes. In your portfolio, write down the tempos at which you can play each major scale without errors. Note your progress as your tempos increase.

Teaching Tip

When recruiting future percussionists, ignore the stereotypes and jokes! Percussionists need excellent aural skills, intelligence, coordination, and self discipline. The ideal percussionist should also be a natural, self-motivated leader with a strong keyboard background.

Create a Rock Drumset Sound within the Concert Percussion Section:
- Hand Cymbals imitate the Hi-Hat (see page 30).
- Bass Drum should be muffled with the hand or knee (see page 31).
- Snare Drum plays rock guitar rhythms.

PERCUSSION ENSEMBLE

66 JUBA

➤ Write out the woodblock part played on CD#1 Track 66.

➤ Improvise a rock style accompaniment using Snare Drum, Bass Drum, Hand Cymbals, and Cowbell.

➤ Name the percussion instrument which keeps the quarter note pulse in
Juba:_____

SEVEN-STROKE ROLL

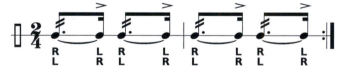

➤ Practice slow-fast-slow.

Primary strokes:

FLAM PARADIDDLE

➤ Practice slow-fast-slow.

YANKEE DOODLE ➤ Play the melody to "Yankee Doodle" by ear on any keyboard mallet instrument in several keys.

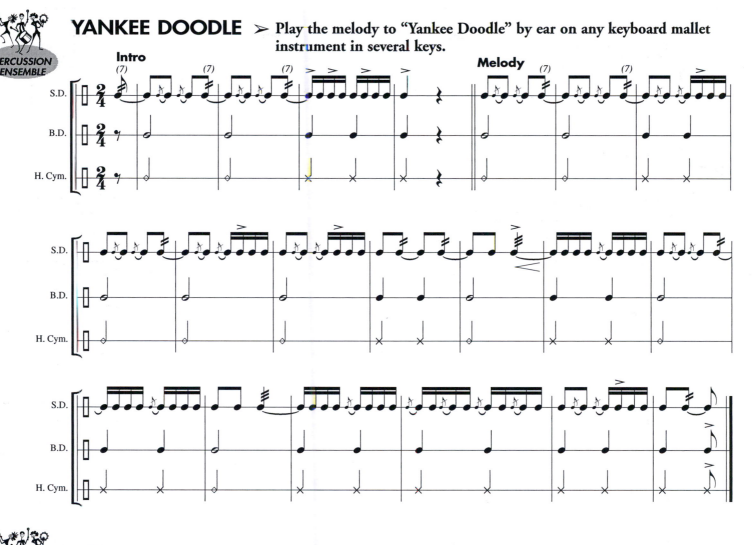

67 YANKEE DOODLE DUET

NEW IDEA!

JAZZ BASICS: THE ii-V-I PROGRESSION

The ii-V-I chord progression is fundamental to jazz music. The ii chord is the Dorian mode. The V chord is the Mixolydian mode, and of course, the I chord signifies the major scale, or the key of the piece. This simple pattern will help you learn to improvise, and improve your overall technique. Transpose it up by half-steps, or use the Circle of Fifths to cover all twelve keys. Record your tempos and progress in your portfolio. Play with a jazz feel (swing eighths), and a rock feel (straight eighths).

68 RUDIMENT REVIEW

➤ There are 8 repeats on CD#1 Track 68 so you can practice this entire page using one track. The tempo gradually increases on each repeat. Bracket and label the rudiments on each exercise.

A. S.D.

B. S.D.

C. S.D.

D. S.D.

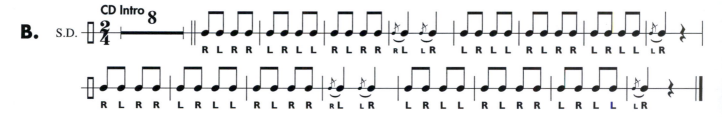

E. S.D.

F. S.D.

G. S.D.

H. S.D.

Skills Assessment • Exercises 63 – 68

SKILLS: **This performance demonstrates:**

SKILLS	10 9	8 7 6	5 4 3	2 1 0
Seven-Stroke Roll • Play Seven-Stroke Roll Ex. on pg. 48 demonstrating primary stroke concept.	Smooth and precise seven-stroke rolls. Correctly demonstrates and understands primary stroke concept.	Slightly inconsistent stick heights on primary strokes resulting in slightly uneven seven-stroke rolls.	Inaccurate seven-stroke rolls caused by incorrect number of bounces on primary strokes, or finishing roll on the wrong stick.	An inability to create seven-stroke rolls. Lacks understanding of primary stroke concept.
Flam Paradiddle • Play Flam Paradiddle rudiment Ex. on pg. 48.	Correct rudiment with both hands striking with same power on flam paradiddle.	Inconsistent stick height/power creates some uneven flam paradiddles.	Inconsistent stick height/power most of the time creates uneven flam paradiddles.	An inability to play flam paradiddles due to lack of practice.
Rock Feel With Concert Band Percussion • Play Ex. 66.	Authentic rock drumset sound.	Unclear rock style because B. D. is open (not muffled), and/or snare drum plays too loudly.	Unconvincing rock style because hand cyms. are played too loosely, and/or B. D. is not muffled correctly, and/or snare drum does not keep steady pulse.	Unawareness of how to create a rock style sound using concert band percussion instruments.
Aural Skills • Play the melody to "Yankee Doodle" on pg. 49.	Accurate rhythmic and melodic performance.	Two to four errors performing melody, rhythms, and/or rests.	Five to eight errors performing melody, rhythms, and/or rests.	More than nine errors performing melody, rhythms, and/or rests.
Castanets and Cowbells • Play Ex. 63 – 66.	Consistently correct and balanced performance technique with clear and precise rhythms.	Overall technique and rhythms are correct. Instruments are too loud, or are out of balance with ensemble phrasing.	Inconsistent sounds due to incorrect technique. Rhythms are not clear or precise.	Incorrect performance technique. Unsteady pulse and out of balance.

PORTFOLIO – Rock Music

Rock music played a vitally important role during the 1960s. In your portfolio, investigate three rock artists/groups from the 1960s. Explain how the music of these groups spoke for many young people during this decade of change in American history.

Comments / Point Total:

Timpani

Skills Summary • Exercise 69 – 71

At the conclusion of Exercises 69 – 71, you will be able to:

- Identify four timpani sizes, parts, and ranges
- Correctly move timpani
- Demonstrate German and French grips on timpani mallets
- Play single stroke notes, rolls, and dampen timpani
- Tune and change pitches
- Arrange percussion ensembles with a timpani part provided
- Play melodies by ear on keyboard percussion

Photo courtesy of Pearl/Adams Percussion.

Teaching Tip

When moving timpani, it's best to walk in front of these large and delicate instruments to prevent damage. Tilt the bowl towards you with the tuning pedal facing upwards. Place your fingers under the rim, and slowly pull the instrument to its new destination. Never set anything on timpani heads except a protective disk and a cover. Be sure your students follow these simple procedures.

TIMPANI

The timpani is one of the most commonly used percussion instruments in contemporary music. Historically, composers used timpani to outline harmonies and to support rhythms in brass instrument parts. Presently, composers use timpani in traditional ways and also as a solo instrument capable of playing intricate rhythms and melodies.

Timpani comes in several sizes. A full set of four comprises drums with bowl sizes of 32", 29", 26", and 23"; the two most common bowl sizes are 29" and 26". Other timpani sizes are available.

TIMPANI RANGES AND SIZES

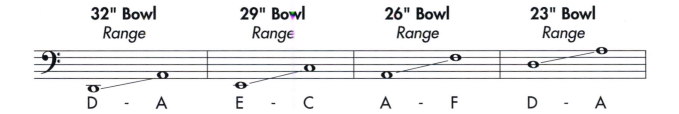

TIMPANI PLAYING POSITION

The timpani are positioned in a semi-circle around the player, with the larger (lower) drums to the left and the smaller (higher) drums to the right. The timpani must be positioned so that the pedals are pointed inward within easy reach of the feet.

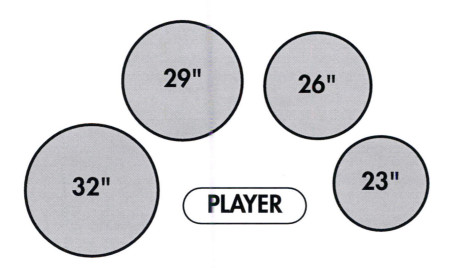

THE STANDING POSITION OR THE SEATED POSITION?

The standing position is recommended for the beginning timpani student. The seated position is used when the player is required to make numerous quick tuning changes.

TIMPANI MALLET GRIPS

The two most common timpani mallet grips are the German and the French. The basic grip point, or fulcrum, on the timpani mallet is the same for both grips: one-third of the mallet length up from the butt end.

GERMAN GRIP

The German Grip is most commonly used by beginning players. It is similar to the matched grip for the snare drum. The mallet is gripped between the thumb and the first finger with the palms facing downward. (The German grip will produce an up-and-down motion of the mallet that is similar to waving good-bye.)

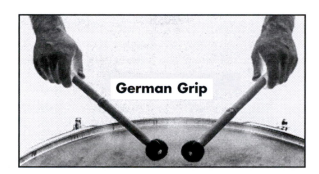

FRENCH GRIP

For the French Grip, the thumbs are positioned on top of the mallets and the fingers are curled under the mallets. (The French grip will produce an up-and-down motion of the mallet that is similar to casting a fishing rod.)

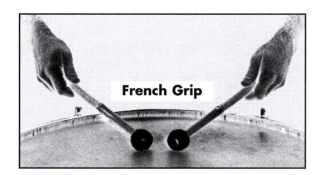

THE TIMPANI STROKE

The beginning player should begin with a full stroke (starts high and ends high). To produce a full, resonant, and characteristic tone of the timpani, the beginning player should experiment with different stroke heights, stroke speeds, and stroke rebounds.

Timpani Stroke Guidelines

- The slower the stroke, the more legato the sound
- A more rapid stroke results in a more staccato sound
- Physical tension results in decreased resonance
- The quicker the rebound the lighter the sound

TIMPANI STRIKING AREA

The timpani striking area is from 2" to 4" from the edge of the bowl, with mallets about 6" apart. The farther apart the mallets, the more legato the sound; the closer together the mallets, the more staccato the sound.

X = Striking Area

TIMPANI TUNING

Timpani tuning requires a good ear (often evidenced as the ability to sing in tune) and the ability to adjust a timpani to match a particular pitch. Students usually begin by learning to adjust the timpani to match a pitch sounded on a keyboard mallet instrument or pitch pipe. More advanced students sometimes use a tuning fork to get a pitch reference for tuning the timpani. Students can improve their tuning proficiency through the study of solfege (a vocal system that assigns syllables to pitches - *do, re, mi, fa, so, la, ti, do*) to represent a major scale that can be sung or heard silently with the mind's ear. Others study music theory to develop improved understanding and tuning proficiency.

To tune a timpani with its pedal tuning mechanism, the player should release the pedal all the way to the lowest pitch of the drum. Next, the player should softly hum the tuning pitch into the drum. Then, the player should depress the pedal to find the desired pitch.

TIMPANI TUNING EXERCISES

1. Sound a B♭ on a keyboard instrument or pitch pipe, release the pedal to the lowest pitch, and tune the large timpani to B♭.

2. Sound an F on a keyboard instrument or pitch pipe, release the pedal to the lowest pitch, and tune the small timpani to F.

3. a) Tune the large drum to F (do).
   b) Sing the ascending syllables (do, re, mi, fa, so), and strike every pitch on the drum.

4. a) Tune the small drum to F (do).
   b) Sing the descending syllables (do, ti, la, so), and strike every pitch on the drum.

TIMPANI ROLL

The timpani roll is one of the most recognized percussion sounds in concert music. It is performed by using an alternating, single-stroke roll. To develop a solid roll technique on the timpani, the beginning player should experiment with different roll heights, roll speeds, and mallets on each drum size. To play soft rolls, keep your stick height low and close to the timpani head. To play louder rolls, use higher stick heights. Practice long crescendos and decrescendos on timpani, aiming for smooth, controlled dynamics. Roll speed is generally slower on large drums, and faster on smaller drums.

TIMPANI ROLL EXERCISES ♩ = 60

TIMPANI DAMPENING
Dampening is used to stop the sound of the timpani. Timpani may be dampened by either the fingers of the hand that played the tone or the fingers of the opposite hand - whichever is most comfortable. The most "fleshy" part of the hand should be used to dampen louder tones. The player should avoid a finger sound or a slapping sound when dampening the timpani. Avoid long fingernails.

TIMPANI DAMPENING EXERCISE 1

(Dampen with the opposite hand that played the note)

Finger Dampening

TIMPANI DAMPENING EXERCISE 2

(Dampen with the opposite hand that played the note)

Dampening can assist the timpanist in matching the articulation, length of notes, and phrasing of the instrumental ensemble. Listen how the timpanist "breathes" with the rest of the ensemble. What phrases do they match? What articulations do they reinforce? How are legato and staccato markings played on timpani? How do these techniques enhance the ensemble?

TIMPANI DAMPENING EXERCISE 3

(Dampen with the hand that played the note)

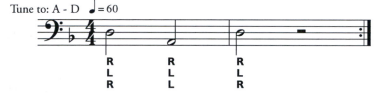

TIMPANI DAMPENING EXERCISE 4

(Dampen with the hand that played the note)

69 SIMPLE GIFTS

70 GO TELL AUNT RHODY

> Play the written timpani part. Create a percussion ensemble for "Go Tell Aunt Rhody" using at least 4 different instruments.

MARCH SLAV

> Write a percussion ensemble arrangement of Tchaikovsky's "March Slav" using this timpani part and at least five other pitched and unpitched percussion instruments.

P. I. Tchaikovsky

ST. ANTHONY CHORALE

> This is a timpani part for the famous "St. Anthony Chorale." Play the chorale on any keyboard percussion instrument by ear. Roll on the half notes as you become more proficient. Remember, musical context is of the utmost importance.

58

71 THE STARS AND STRIPES FOREVER

➤ CD#1's final track (71) provides you with a chance to accompany a concert band playing one of our nation's greatest marches, *The Stars and Stripes Forever,* by John Philip Sousa. As always, play musically and give special attention to the written dynamics.

Skills Assessment • Exercises 69 – 71

SKILLS: **This performance demonstrates:**

SKILLS	10 9	8 7 6	5 4 3	2 1 0
Timpani • Identify and position timpani parts, ranges, sizes.	Correct identification, positioning, and moving of all timpani parts, ranges, sizes.	Two to four errors in identifying timpani parts, sizes, ranges, set-up, and/or moving.	Four to six errors in identifying timpani parts, sizes, ranges, set-up, and/or moving.	Could not identify timpani parts or ranges. Set-up and moving were incorrect.
Grip (Pg. 54) • Demonstrate German and French grips.	Correct hand and thumb positions on German (down) and French (up) grips.	Mostly accurate, but palms and thumbs occasionally rotate upward or inward.	Incorrect thumb position most of the time on German (down) and/or French (up) grips.	Inability to demonstrate the difference between German and French grips.
Strokes, Rolls, and Dampening • Play Ex. 69 – 70 • Play Ex. on pages 55 and 56.	Correct strokes and strike area. Stick height is equal between hands creating smooth and even rolls. Dampening is quiet, precise.	Stick height is, at times, inconsistent (too high/too low) causing uneven dynamics, notes, and rhythms. Some dampening is late and/or too loud.	Incorrect stick height creates sounds which are out of musical context. Dampening is often late and/or too loud (fingers).	Inability to play in correct striking area or with matching stick height. Musical context is absent.
Tuning Procedure • Play Ex. on pages 55 and 57.	Excellent ability to hear and sing pitches and tune timpani correctly.	Minor errors in singing intervals and/or tuning (slightly sharp/flat).	Difficulty in hearing and singing most new pitches, and adjusting timpani.	Inability to hear and sing matching pitches. Tuning timpani is not successful.
Percussion Ensemble Arrangements • Arrange percussion ensembles on page 57.	Arranged parts match timpani phrasing and enhance musical context.	Slightly compromised musical context due to arranged parts not matching timpani parts.	A complete arrangement, but musical context suffers.	Little or no sense of phrase or shape between written timpani part and arrangements, or arrangements are incomplete.

PORTFOLIO – Timpani "Roles"

Find at least three examples of musical "roles" given to timpani by various composers, including melodic parts, dramatic (describe the effect and how it is achieved), and harmonic (describe how timpani are used to reinforce harmonies and/or cadences). Include titles, composers, and information about why the pieces were written, if available.

Comments / Point Total:

SECTION 2 · CD #2 DRUMSET AND WORLD PERCUSSION

Drumset, Tuning, Coordination, Swing

Skills Summary • Exercises 1 – 11

At the conclusion of Exercises 1 – 11, you will be able to:

- Identify parts and set up a drumset
- Play a basic jazz swing pattern on drumset
- Use snare drum brushes
- Develop basic two-way coordination
- Develop basic three-way coordination
- Develop basic four-way coordination

Basic Five-Piece Setup

DRUMSET NOTATION KEY

Hi-Hat w/foot	Bass Drum	Floor Tom	Snare Drum	Cross Stick	Mounted Tom	Cowbell	Hi-Hat Closed w/Stick	Hi-Hat Open	Hi-Hat Closed	Ride Cym.	Ride Cym. on Bell	Crash Cym.
						◆	✕	○	+	✕	⊗	✱
✕	●	●	●	⊗	●							

BASIC 5-PIECE DRUM KIT SETUP*

The 5-piece drum kit includes a bass drum, snare drum, two mounted toms, one floor tom, two cymbals, and a hi-hat.

The overall concept is to set up for comfort! The drums and cymbals should be set up where everything is within easy reach. When seated at the drum throne, the kit should resemble sitting at a table, with everything within easy reach. So, let's "set the table."

THE THRONE
The setup process starts with the throne or stool. The height should reflect a comfortable sitting position where the thighs are parallel to the floor or a bit angled downward. When you place the feet on the pedals, your legs should be just past a 45-degree angle. See diagram.

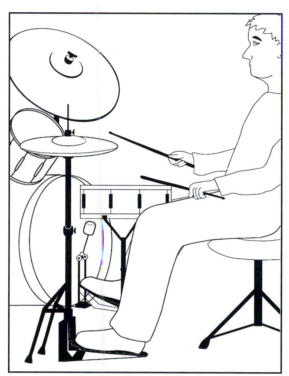

SNARE DRUM
The snare drum should be at a comfortable playing height, so the arms are level with the drum or just dipping slightly. Many young players setup with the snare drum much too low, which limits the hands.

TOMS
The mounted toms should be positioned where you can pivot off the snare drum and strike the toms easily. The angle of the drums shouldn't be radical in order to play all the different parts of the drum. The floor tom should be about the same height as the snare drum, perhaps slightly lower.

CYMBALS
The ride cymbal should be positioned where the player can simply extend the arm (like a handshake) and the cymbal is right there! There should be no reaching for any cymbal because this will cause fatigue. Young players often have large sized tom toms mounted on the bass drum forcing the placement of the ride cymbal off to the extreme right of the player. This will cause the player to have to contort the hand in order to play the cymbal.

SUMMARY
Set up the drum kit around your body. Don't try and adapt a cool looking setup of another drummer. From time to time, it is a good idea to evaluate your setup to see if your body has changed. As players get older, they seem to sit higher.

*For a detailed setup guide, please refer to "How to Set Up Your Drumset" by Dave Black, published by Alfred.

TUNING*

Proper tuning of the drums is fundamental to achieving a good sound on the drums. However, there are many variables that make the process more involved. First of all, make sure that the drumheads are in good shape, preferably new. The proper head selection is important when trying to get a sound. (Rock, jazz, and studio sounds all require different types of sounds.)

Another variable is the bearing edge of the drum. Make sure that the edge of the drum is nice and smooth with no "dings" taken out of it.

Finally, the rim has a lot to do with the tuning process. Many older drumsets have bent or dented rims which will always compromise the tuning process.

TUNING THE SNARE DRUM

Tune the snare drum starting with the batter head first. Start with tension rod at 12 o'clock, and moving clockwise, hand tighten all around the drum. Then, tighten each post 1/2 turn until the head is firm. You can now spot check by tapping the head with a drumstick (snares off) about two inches from the tension rod, seeing that the pitch is consistent around the drum.

The bottom head on the snare drum is tuned in the same manner but the pitch of it is usually higher than the batter head.

TUNING TOM-TOMS

The toms are tuned in the same manner. Experiment with the pitch of the top and bottom heads. Some drummers prefer the bottom head lower for a "fall-off" kind of sound, while others like a looser top head for a softer feeling drum. The pitches for the toms should create intervals so that contrast is achieved.

TUNING THE BASS DRUM

A two-headed bass drum can be tuned in a variety of ways. By tuning the batter head or back head fairly loose but not wrinkled and then tuning the front head pretty tight, it provides a bass drum sound that has pitch and punch; a good combination for most musical settings. A felt strip can be used to take out unwanted rings or overtones.

TUNING PITCHES

Every drum has a pitch range where it sounds the best and resonates freely. Although you can't really put pitches on drums, here are some good starting pitches for tuning:

10" tom - F

12" tom - D

13" tom - B♭

16" tom - F

Snare Drum - E♭ - G (Use a higher pitch for more rock or fusion drumming)

Bass Drum - E♭ (before muffling)

*For a detailed tuning guide, please refer to "How To Tune Your Drums" by Dave Black, published by Alfred.

DRUMSET PLAYING TECHNIQUE

RIDE CYMBAL

The ride cymbal grip is very similar to the French timpani grip. Extend your hand, like you're going to shake hands with someone and then put the stick between your thumb and first finger, creating a fulcrum. The thumb will be pressing down on the first joint of the first finger. The other three fingers are then placed on the stick and consequently follow the stick. The cymbal is struck about two inches from the edge of the cymbal. The height of the ride cymbal stroke should be approximately four inches, depending on tempo and volume.

● **The exercise numbers in Section 2 match the CD#2 Track numbers.**

❶ RIDE CYMBAL BEATS

➤ On CD#2 Track 1, Steve Houghton will play each single measure ride cymbal beat pattern with you four times. Then, you'll only hear an open click. Keep playing the pattern another four times on your own, and then move to the next ride cymbal beat pattern. Steve will play the next ride cymbal beat pattern with you four times. Stay with the click.

Quarter Note Ride Beat

Eighth Note Ride Beat

Jazz Ride Beat

Jazz Ride Beat – Triplet Feel

BASS DRUM

The bass drum can be played with various techniques, however the author suggests a "heel down" approach where the foot simply rests on the foot board.

Note: Many students play with the "heel up" using the toe or ball of the foot. This approach seems to work well with loud volume music, but will take more time to develop the desired finesse and control.

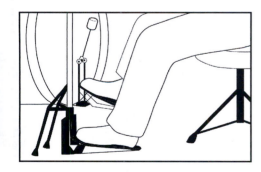

❷ BASS DRUM

➤ **Play Exercise 2 with bass drum model on CD#2 Track 2 twice. Then, repeat Exercise 2 two more times on your own. Stay with the click.**

Play 4 times.

HI-HAT

Various techniques can also be used on the hi-hat. A solid technique for beginning players is called the "rocking motion" technique. This involves a rocking motion with the foot, stepping down on beats 2 and 4 (toe) and then rocking up on the heel on beats 1 and 3.

3 **HI-HAT**

➤ **Play along with CD#2 Track 3 two times with the hi-hat model. Then, play two more times on your own. Stay with the click.**

SNARE DRUM

Use the same snare drum technique you've been practicing.

TWO-WAY COORDINATION

The following exercises will help develop independence between the limbs, which is essential when playing the drumset. First, we will focus on two-way coordination between the ride cymbal and snare drum. The ride cymbal will play an ostinato ride pattern against various snare drum rhythms. Then, the bass drum will play rhythms against the cymbal ostinato.

Ride Cymbal Ostinato

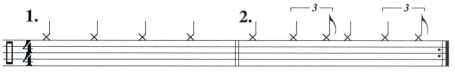

4 ➤ **Play the ride cymbal with your right hand, and the snare drum with your left hand.**

SNARE DRUM EXERCISES

➤ **Play Examples A-F three times each with CD#2 Track 4. The ride cymbal fades out so you can play the ostinato on your own. Stay with the click.**

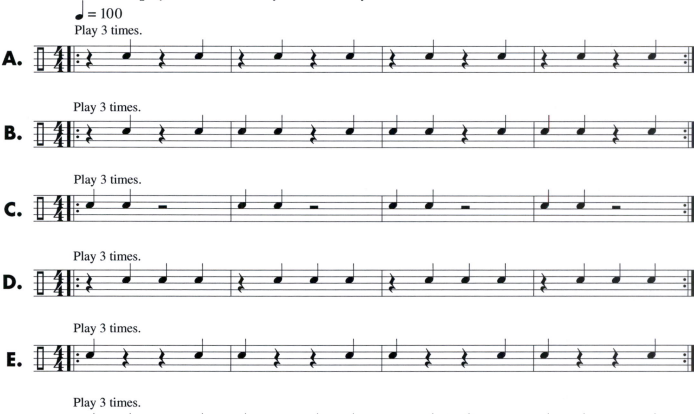

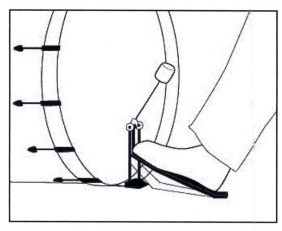

Correct right foot position for bass drum.

Incorrect right foot position for bass drum.
Don't play like this!

Ride Cymbal Ostinato

5 ➤ Play the bass drum with your right foot, and the ride cymbal with your right hand.

BASS DRUM EXERCISES

➤ Play Examples A-H three times each with CD#2 Track 5. The ride cymbal fades out so you can play the ostinato on your own. Stay with the click.

♩ = 100
Play 3 times.

A.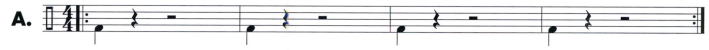

Play 3 times.

B.

Play 3 times.

C.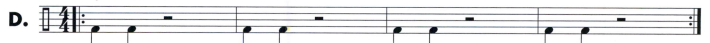

Play 3 times.

D.

Play 3 times.

E.

Play 3 times.

F.

Play 3 times.

G.

Play 3 times.

H.

THREE-WAY COORDINATION

When you are comfortable with two-way coordination on the previous pages, play the snare drum exercises on page 64 with a hi-hat on beats 2 and 4. Practice exercises A-F until you are comfortable with three-way coordination. Use both ride cymbal ostinato patterns with **CD#2 Track 4**. Stay with the click.

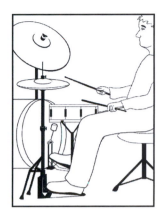

Here's Example A using Ride Cymbal Ostinato Pattern #1:

> ➤ **Which limb plays ride cymbal?**_____

> ➤ **Which limb plays snare drum?**_____

> ➤ **Which limb plays hi-hat?**_____

Now, go back to the Bass Drum exercises on page 65. Play the bass drum exercises (A-H) adding snare drum on beats 2 and 4. Repeat Exercises A-H until you are comfortable with three-way coordination. Use both ride cymbal ostinato patterns with **CD#2 Track 5**. Stay with the click.

Here's Example A using Ride Cymbal ostinato Pattern #1:

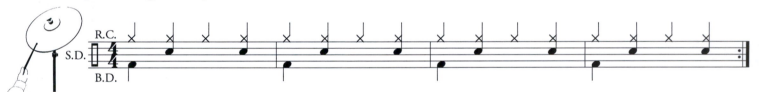

> ➤ **Which arm plays ride cymbal?**_____

> ➤ **Which foot plays bass drum?**_____

> ➤ **Which limb plays snare drum?**_____

PORTFOLIO – Drumset Artists

What characteristics define a good drummer? As you practice Two-Way Coordination exercises, listen how you balance one sound with another. Then, while practicing Three-Way Coordination, experiment with different volumes. Listen to recordings of at least five different drumset players performing a variety of jazz styles, and be aware of the balance, technique, sensitivies, and highly musical nature of playing drumset. Write your observations in your portfolio.

Teaching Tip

Be a judge in your state's organized solo, ensemble, and concert group music festivals. The experience will enhance your own teaching abilities, allow you to meet other colleagues, discuss music education issues, and provide you with additional income. Most importantly, you'll be making a difference in the lives of every young student who performs for you. Take this responsibility very seriously.

FOUR-WAY COORDINATION

To develop four-way coordination, practice Exercises A-G while playing each of the jazz beat ostinatos. Play number one until it is comfortable and then try number two, etc.

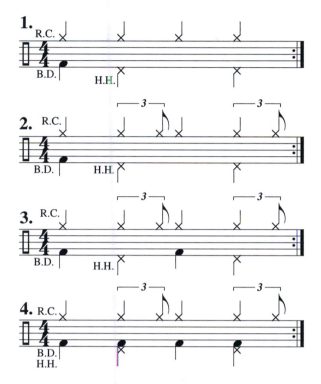

6 ➢ Play Exercises A-G three times each with CD#2 Track 6. Stay with the click throughout.

7 HE'S GOT THE WHOLE WORLD IN HIS HANDS

➤ **Play the melody by ear and improvise harmonies on any keyboard percussion instrument.**

NEW IDEA!

BRUSH STROKE

Think of the drum as the face of a clock. Lay the brushes on the drum and move them in circles as indicated. Cross at 12 O'clock on beats 1, 2, 3, and 4.

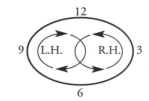

8 GLOW WORM

(CD Intro)

9 WORRIED MAN BLUES

(CD Intro)

➤ **Improvise over the chords on any keyboard percussion instrument.**

PORTFOLIO – 12-Bar Blues

The 12-bar blues are a fundamental part of music history. The Blues evolved from the music of Black Americans in the mid-1800s. Listen to the recordings of at least three Blues artists. Describe what you hear – the chord progressions, the types of lyrics, the solos, the various tempos, and most importantly, listen to the drummer. When do the drummer's ride cymbal beats align with the bass player's notes? Name five Blues artists who helped define this form and style. Print your research in your portfolio. (CD#2 Tracks 4, 5, and 6 are 12-bar Blues.)

10 WHEN THE SAINTS GO MARCHING IN

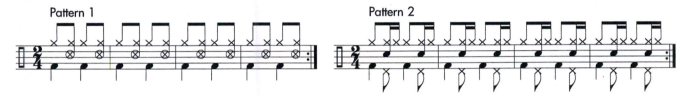

➤ **Drumset: Play Pattern 1 the first time through, then play Pattern 2 on the repeat. Add fills where you feel they are needed.**

➤ **Keyboard Percussion: Play the melody to "When the Saints Go Marching In" with CD#2 Track 10. On the repeat, improvise a part with the other Dixieland artists on the recording.**

11 HELLO MY BABY

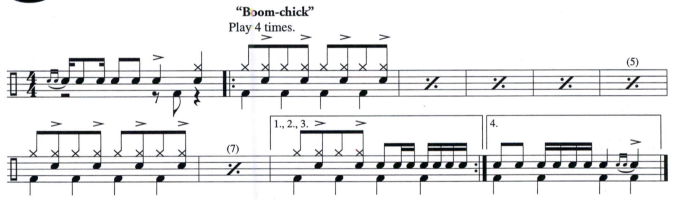

➤ **Listen how the accents enhance the "boom-chick" style of this lively piece. Imitate this style when you play "Hello My Baby" with CD#2 Track 11.**

PORTFOLIO – The Drummer's Role in Jazz, Swing, and Rock Bands

Find recordings of three jazz swing bands and three rock bands. Concentrate on listening to the drumset player. What specific things does the drummer do to enhance the musical context of the piece? For example, is the bass drum played heavier or lighter in rock music compared to swing? What about the snare drum? What beats do both styles emphasize? Compare cymbal sounds in rock bands and jazz swing bands. How do drummers help singers and instrumentalists in each style? Be as specific as possible in your portfolio.

Skills Assessment • Exercises 1 – 11

SKILLS: **This performance demonstrates:**

SKILLS:	10 9	8 7 6	5 4 3	2 1 0
Drumset • Identify instruments and set up a drumset.	Correct identification and set-up of drumset.	Two to four errors in identifying and/or set-up of drumset.	Four to six errors in identifying and/or set-up of drumset.	Could not identify or set-up drumset.
Two-Way Coordination • Play pg. 64, 65 R.C. and S.D., R.C. and B.D.	Accurate and precise coordination between R.C., S.D. and R.C., B.C.	R.C. occasionally does not align with S.D. and/or B.D. B.D. is sometimes too heavy.	R.C. and B.D. and/or S.D. rhythms do not align most of the time. B.D. is too loud and heavy.	Inability to play two-way coordination on drumset.
Three-Way Coordination • Play pg. 66 R.C., S.D., Hi-Hat R.C., B.D., Hi-Hat.	Clear H.H. on 2 and 4 with consistent beat alignment with R.C. S.D., B.D. are well balanced with consistently accurate rhythms.	H.H. is not always strong enough on 2 and 4. H.H. and R.C. do not always align (early/late), S.D. is sometimes too loud, B.D. is sometimes too loud.	H.H. is weak (step down harder) on 2 and 4, R.C. stroke is inconsistent, and/or S.D. is too loud or rhythms are not accurate, B.D. is too loud/inaccurate.	Inability to play three-way coordination on drumset.
Four-Way Coordination • Play pg. 67 Ex. A-G.	Clear H.H. on 2 and 4 with consistent beat alignment with R.C. Snare drum and B.D. are well balanced with consistently accurate rhythms.	H.H. is not always strong enough on 2 and 4, H.H. and R.C. do not always align (early/late), S.D. is sometimes too loud, B.D. is sometimes too loud.	H.H. is weak (step down harder) on 2 and 4, R.C. stroke is inconsistent (stick height, dynamics, or striking area), S.D. is too loud or rhythms are not accurate, B.D. is too loud/inaccurate.	Inability to play four-way coordination on drumset.
Jazz Swing Pattern with S.D. Cross Stick • Play Ex. 9 and 10.	Accurate jazz swing sound. Cross stick produces a "fat" sound.	H.H. is not always strong enough on 2 and 4, H.H. and R.C. do not always align (early/late), cross stick sound is inconsistent, B.D. is often too heavy.	H.H. is weak (step down harder) on 2 and 4, R.C. stroke is inconsistent, cross stick rhythms are out of time, B.D. is too loud/inaccurate.	Inability to play jazz swing pattern with snare drum cross stick.

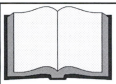

PORTFOLIO – Drumsets

Who were the first drumset players? Who built the first drumset? How many manufacturers build drumsets? Find the answers to these questions, and include your findings in your portfolio.

Rock, Hard Rock, Rhythm and Blues

Skills Summary • Exercises 12 – 22

At the conclusion of Exercises 12 – 22, you will be able to:

- Play a basic rock groove on drumset
- Define and demonstrate a drumset fill
- Play a $\frac{12}{8}$ rhythm and blues groove
- Play the melody to "Scotland the Brave" by ear.

ROCK

Rock music became the new form of popular music in the late 1950s and the early 1960s. In this style, beats 2 and 4 are accented on the snare drum, and straight eighth notes are played on the hi-hat or ride cymbal.

ROCK GROOVES

12 BASIC ROCK GROOVE

➤ When playing the hi-hat with your right hand, keep your left foot down to tightly close the hi-hat. Play snare drum rhythms with your left hand.

13 BASIC ROCK GROOVE (♩♩♩♩)

14 BASIC ROCK GROOVE (♪♪♪♪)

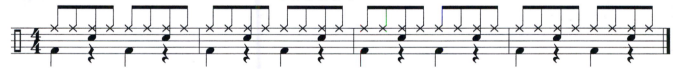

Fill

Drumset players are often asked to play "fills." A **fill** is a short, improvised solo played in the style of the piece. Drum fills are used to complete a phrase, enhance a transition, or allow instrumentalists or singers to breathe. Most importantly, drumset fills must always enhance the musical context of the piece. Listen to CD#2 Track 15 and identify the fills you hear. On what beats do fills often occur?

15 BASIC ROCK GROOVE (With Fills)

➤ Transcribe the fill bars:

> Play Exercise 16 with CD#2 Track 16. On the repeat, you're on your own. Stay with the click.

16 GROOVE DEVELOPMENT ROUTINE #1

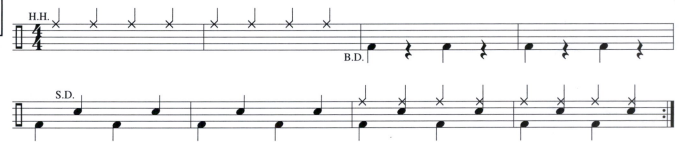

> Play Exercise 17 with CD#2 Track 17. On the repeat, you're on your own. Stay with the click.

17 MEDIUM ROCK PLAY ALONG #1

♩ = 96

Teaching Tip

Your music library of recordings should provide you and your students with a varied collection of different styles of music. Here is a recommended list of recordings for your home and school music libraries:

Jazz

Satchmo At Symphony Hall	Louis Armstrong
Kind of Blue	Miles Davis
Moanin'	Art Blakey
Brown/Roach Inc.	Max Roach
At The Pershing	Ahmad Jamal

Brazilian

Getz/Gilberto	Stan Getz
The Legendary Joao Gilberto	Joao Gilberto
Tom and Elis	Antonio Carlos Jobim
Oceano	Sergio Mendes
Braziliero	Toots Thielemans

Afro-Cuban

Master Sessions	Cachao
The Best of Irakere	Irakere
Palmas	Eddie Palmieri
Top Percussion	Tito Puente
Afro-Cuban Fantasy	Poncho Sanchez

Funk-Fusion

In Modern Times	Spyro Gyra
Live Wires	Yellowjackets
Voices	Mike Stern
The Zone	Dave Weckl
Crush	Richard Elliot

➤ Play Exercise 18 with CD#2 Track 18. On the repeat, you're on your own. Stay with the click.

18 GROOVE DEVELOPMENT ROUTINE #2

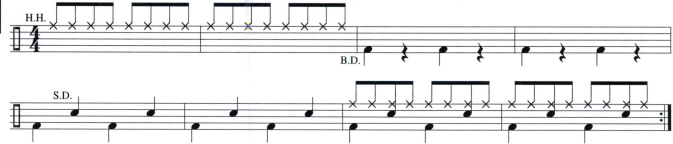

➤ Play Exercise 19 with CD#2 Track 19. On the repeat, you're on your own. Stay with the click.

19 MEDIUM ROCK PLAY ALONG #2

Alternative Bass Drum Patterns

HARD ROCK

Popular music originating in America and England in the 1970s. Hard rock bands include a bass player, at least one guitarist, a lead singer, at least one percussionist, and very often, a keyboard specialist.

➤ **Write the guitar chord changes above the staff. Play the melody to "Scotland the Brave" by ear on any keyboard mallet percussion instrument, and roll on every note.**

20 SCOTLAND THE BRAVE

PORTFOLIO – Rock Music

Rock music refers to most popular music recorded anytime after the mid-to-late 1950's. Various artists pioneered and defined specific styles of rock music. Listen to recordings of at least three artists from each rock style listed below, and write your observations of the differences of each style in your portfolio. Include stylistic or artistic influences you hear in these styles:

- Rock 'n' Roll
- Rock
- Hard Rock
- Country Rock

RHYTHM AND BLUES

Rhythm and Blues, commonly known as "R&B," originated from African American musicians. The recordings of B. B. King, Ray Charles, and Muddy Waters helped define this style, and continue to influence current composers and performing artists.

$\frac{12}{8}$ HAND AND FEET EXERCISES

21 ➤ Exercises A - C will help you develop the skills needed to play Rhythm and Blues (R&B) style music. Practice each one bar example until you are proficient, and then move on to the next measure. Play along with CD#2 Track 21.

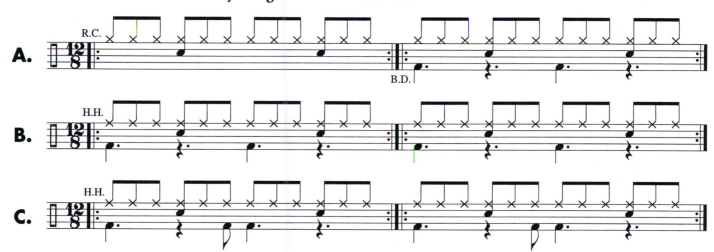

➤ Exercises D-F should be played three times each with CD#2 Track 21.

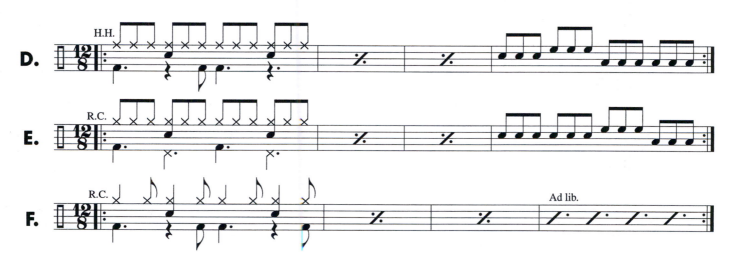

PORTFOLIO – Rhythm and Blues (R&B) Music

Listen to and list at least four different R&B artists/groups. In your portfolio, write down the characteristics of what you hear in R&B music: time signatures, lyrics, and rhythms which help define this style of American music.

➤ Write the ride cymbal rhythms played in a jazz swing style:_____

➤ Write the ride cymbal rhythms played in a rock groove:_____

➤ Write the ride cymbal rhythms played in the R&B style:_____

22 AMERICA THE BEAUTIFUL

➢ Who is the popular, blind R&B jazz singer who sang and recorded a version of "America" in this style?_____

Skills Assessment • Exercises 12 – 22

SKILLS: **This performance demonstrates:**

	10 9	8 7 6	5 4 3	2 1 0
Rock Groove • Play Ex. 17.	Even, firm, consistent H.H. strokes, S.D., B.D. dynamics, rhythms are equal to and aligned.	Occasionally uneven H.H. Striking area wavers, B.D. is sometimes too loud. S.D. backbeats do not always align with beat.	Incorrect H.H. (hitting w/different parts of the stick, not stepping down firmly enough), B.D. is too loud, S.D. rhythms are late.	Inability to play basic rock groove with quarter notes.
Rock Groove • Play Ex. 19.	Even, firm, consistent H.H. strokes, S.D., B.D. dynamics, rhythms are equal to and aligned.	Occasionally uneven H.H. Striking area wavers, B.D. is sometimes too loud. S.D. backbeats do not always align with beat.	Incorrect H.H. (hitting w/different parts of the stick, not stepping down firmly enough), B.D. is too loud, S.D. rhythms are late.	Inability to play basic rock groove with quarter notes.
Rock Groove with Fills • Play Ex. 20.	Authentic, well-balanced rock groove. Fills are in time, and always enhance musical context.	Occasionally unbalanced rock groove (S.D. too soft, beats don't always align). Fills do not enhance music, and are occasionally not in tempo.	Incorrect rock groove (H.H. is too soft, B.D. is heavy, S.D. rhythms are late). Fills are not in tempo, or do not include enough drumset sounds.	Inability to play basic rock groove with fills.
Aural Skills • Write in guitar chords on Ex. 20.	Accurate chord changes noted.	Two to four errors on written chord changes.	Five to eight errors on written chord changes.	More than nine errors on written chord changes.
R&B Groove • Play Ex. 21, 22.	Accurate R and B groove. H.H. is even, cross stick produces "fat" sound. B.D. and R.C. are precise.	H.H. is sometimes uneven due to inconsistent stick position. Cross stick sound is uneven. R.C. and B.D. are too heavy.	H.H. is uneven with little sense of time. B.D. is inaccurate and too light. Cross stick rhythm is out of time.	Inability to play R&B groove.

PORTFOLIO – Research Drumset Books

There are numerous drumset books available, such as *Drum Sessions,* by Peter O'Gorman, and *Drumset Performer,* by Steve Houghton. Beginning Level Style Compilation - *Essential Styles, Books 1 and 2,* by Steve Houghton. Additional drumset books are listed in the Resource Section of this book. Become familiar with these books for your future use with students. Print your findings in your portfolio.

Comments / Point Total:

Latin

Skills Summary • Exercises 23 – 28

At the conclusion of Exercises 23 – 28, you will be able to:

- Play a basic Latin style groove on drumset
- Arrange a Latin style groove on drumset
- Play melodies by ear on keyboard percussion
- Play and listen to Calypso and Bossa Nova music

NEW STYLE!

Latin

Latin American music is dance music. Drumset players create Latin grooves by playing straight eighth notes on ride cymbal and dotted quarter/eighth note rhythms on bass drum. The snare drum cross stick rhythms imitate the claves rhythms. The Bossa Nova is a basic Latin groove.

 **23 CHEATER BOSSA**

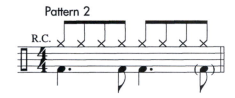 **24 BOSSA NOVA**

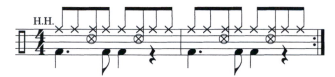

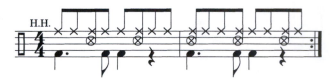

> **What is the difference between "Cheater Bossa" and "Bossa Nova"? Listen to the balance of all four instruments on Tracks 23 and 24. Imitate this style when you play Latin styles.**

25 BOSSA NOVA GROOVE

> **Practice "Bossa Nova Groove" with CD#2 using the Cheater Bossa or the Bossa Nova patterns. Listen to the fills and create your own Bossa Groove with the CD. Other players should play characteristic Latin rhythms. Rotate parts.**

NEW SKILL!

LATIN INDEPENDENCE EXERCISES

> Play Pattern 1 with Exercises A-H along with CD#2 Track 26. Then, play the same exercises using Pattern 2.

 26 LATIN PLAY ALONG #1

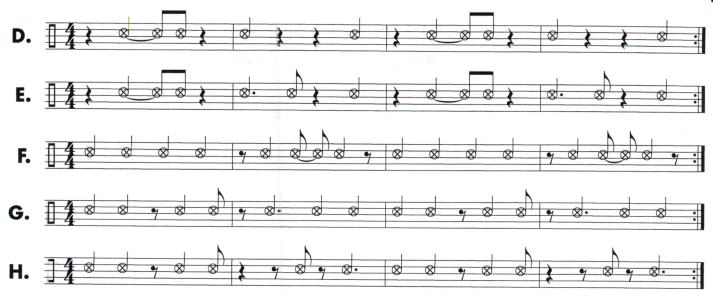

27 LATIN PLAY ALONG #2 (faster)

➤ Practice Latin Independence Exercises with exercises A-H using CD#2 Track 27.

NEW STYLE!

CALYPSO

Music with origins in Trinidad. Calypso music is often syncopated and energetic.

PERCUSSION ENSEMBLE

28 JAMAICAN FAREWELL

Drumset: Play the Calypso pattern throughout the piece. Listen carefully to the style, technique, and balance of each drumset instrument on the CD. Imitate these elements.

Snares off

➤ **Keyboard Percussion:** Play the melody to "Jamaican Farewell" by ear with CD#2 Track 28. On the repeat, improvise a part with the other Calypso artists on the recording.

Skills Assessment • Exercises 23 – 28

SKILLS:	This performance demonstrates:			
Latin Groove • Play Ex. 23 – 27.	10 9 Well balanced Latin style including cross-stick played at the correct position and volume, rhythms are consistently accurate, B.D. and H.H. are controlled and consistently accurate.	8 7 6 Cross-stick sound is occasionally too thin due to playing too far down on the stick, B.D. and H.H. are occasionally too loud, rhythms are not always accurate or right on the beat.	5 4 3 Cross-stick sound is too thin due to playing too far down on the stick, B.D. and H.H. are too loud, rhythms are inaccurate and not on the beat. Overall volume is not consistent.	2 1 0 Inability to play four way coordination using a Latin groove.
Aural Skills and Improvisation • Play Ex. 28.	10 9 Accurate rhythms, melodies, and harmonies. Improvised exercises had sense of composition, and tension/release.	8 7 6 Four to six errors performing melodies by ear. Improvised exercises lacked tension/release, but were complete.	5 4 3 Five to eight errors performing melodies by ear. Improvised exercises lacked ability to hear chord changes.	2 1 0 More than nine errors performing melodies by ear. Improvised exercises were not completed.

World Percussion
African, Afro-Cuban, Brazilian

AFRICAN

Skills Summary • Exercises 29 – 37

At the conclusion of page 96, you will be able to:

- Identify and correctly play Dawuro (African Bell), Gankogui (African Double Bell), Shekere, Djembe, Djun-Djun, Congas, Bongos, Surdo, Agogo Bells, Pandiero, Tamborim, Timbales, and Ganza
- Play authentic African, Afro-Cuban, and Brazilian rhythms
- Improvise accompaniments in African, Afro-Cuban, and Brazilian styles
- Improvise on keyboard percussion using the F Minor Pentatonic and F Blues scales
- Arrange a percussion ensemble using instruments introduced on pages 80 - 96

PORTFOLIO – African Music, Instruments, and Culture

The Dawuro, Gankogui, Shekere, Djembe, and Djun-Djun are all instruments used in African music. Find recordings of two African musicians or groups. Listen carefully to the percussion. What rhythms do you hear played by various instruments? Why is this music an important part of African culture? What does this music say to you?

DAWURO (AFRICAN BELL)

The Dawuro (daw-you-row) is a boat-shaped iron bell played with a hard stick. (The cowbell, played with a drumstick, is an adequate substitute for the Dawuro.)

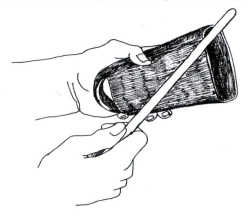

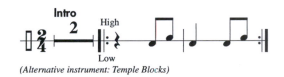

GANKOGUI (AFRICAN DOUBLE BELL)

The Gankogui (gan-koo-gee) is an iron double bell that produces a high tone and a low tone. It is played with a wooden stick.

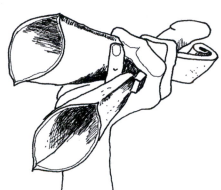

(Alternative instrument: Temple Blocks)

SHEKERE

The Shekere (sheah-ker-reh) is an African-derived rattle made from a gourd and covered with a loose net of beads. Sounds are produced by a combination of striking with the left hand and shaking and bouncing in both up and down and circular motions with the right hand. A bass tone can be produced by striking the bottom of the gourd.

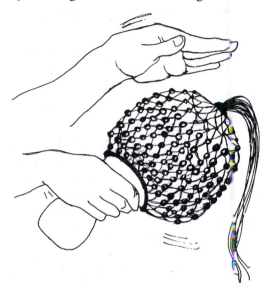

(Alternative instrument: Maracas)

DJEMBE

The Djembe (jem-beh) originated in West Africa. It can be played three ways: strapped to the player, placed on a stand, or set on the ground and held at a slight angle between the legs.

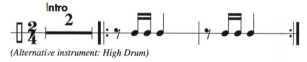

(Alternative instrument: High Drum)

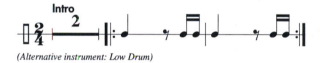

(Alternative instrument: Low Drum)

Two basic strokes employed *ad lib.* produce the characteristic sound of the Djembe:

1. The Bass Tone is produced by striking the drum in the middle of the head with a bouncing stroke of the entire hand.

Bass Tone

2. The Open Tone is produced by striking the rim of the drum with a rebounding stroke of relaxed and fully extended fingers.

Open Tone

DJUN-DJUN

The Djun-Djun (joon-joon) is another drum originating in West Africa. Considered the African bass drum, it lays the foundation for African High Life drumming. The Djun-Djun is set on the ground and played with a wooden or hard felt beater.

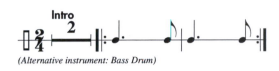

(Alternative instrument: Bass Drum)

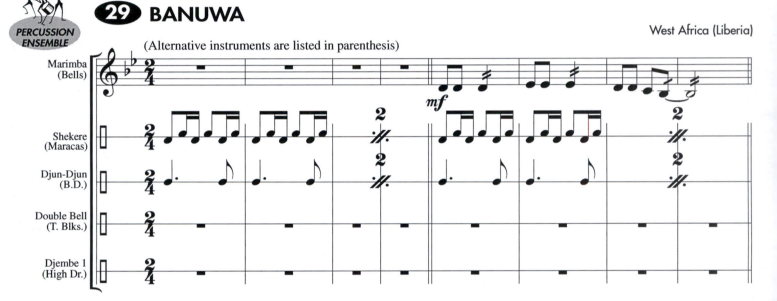

29 BANUWA

West Africa (Liberia)

CAXIXI

The Caxixi (kah-shee-shee) are weaved baskets filled with beads, pebbles, or beans. They are grasped by small handles attached to the top of each basket. Rhythm patterns are created by shaking one or more in each hand.

30 AFRICAN FAREWELL

Sierra Leone

84

 31 EXTENDED AFRICAN PLAY ALONG

➤ Using the rhythms on the instruments you've just learned, play along with CD#2 Track 31. Listen how these simple rhythm patterns create an infectious African groove with the vocal lines.

PERCUSSION ENSEMBLE

Label the following:

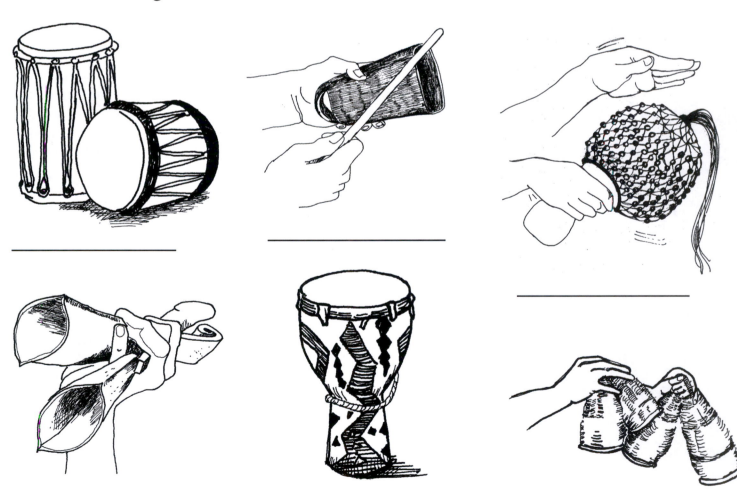

_____   _____   _____

_____   _____   _____

AFRO-CUBAN

> **PORTFOLIO – Afro-Cuban Music, Instruments, and Culture**
> The Guiro, Timbales, Congas, and Claves are used in Afro-Cuban music. Find recordings of two Afro-Cuban musicians or groups. Listen carefully to the percussion. What rhythms do you hear played by various instruments? Why is this music called Afro-Cuban? Name an American composer who has used Afro-Cuban influences in a composition, and name the composition. What does this music say to you?

GUIRO

The Guiro is a gourd with ridges carved into it. It is played by scraping the ridges with a thin wooden stick. The Guiro is held by placing the thumb and index finger into the set of carved holes. The characteristic sound of the instrument is produced by a series of alternating up and down strokes.

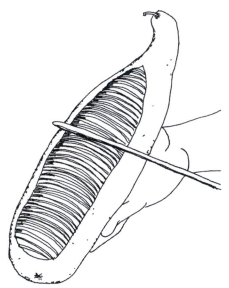

(Alternative instrument: S.D./Rim)

TIMBALES

The Timbales, originating in Cuba, are a pair of single-headed drums mounted on a stand. They are played with thin timbale sticks in combination with hand dampening. The large timbale is placed on the player's left. The sticks are held with a matched grip.

> ➤ **Timbale players often improvise stylistic fills at cadence points. Watch for *Ad lib.***

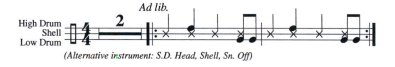

(Alternative instrument: S.D. Head, Shell, Sn. Off)

CONGAS

The Conga Drums are long single-headed drums thatt were brought to the Caribbean islands by Africans. They can be played singly or in combinations of two or more drums. Traditionally, they are played in a seated position with the drums held between the legs. They may also be placed on a stand.

➤ Conga players often improvise stylistic fills at cadence points. Watch for *Ad lib.*

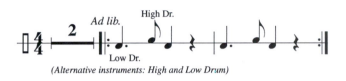

(Alternative instruments: High and Low Drum)

Two basic strokes, employed *ad lib.* produce the characteristic sound of the Conga drums:

1. The Bass Tone is produced by striking the drum in the middle of the head with a bouncing stroke of the entire hand.

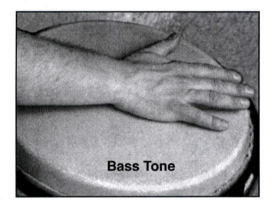

2. The Open Tone is produced by striking the rim of the drum with a rebounding stroke of relaxed and fully extended fingers.

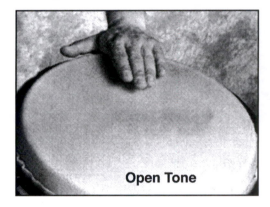

F MINOR PENTATONIC SCALE

➤ The F Minor Pentatonic scale can be used to improvise rhythmic and melodic variations on "Latin Blues." Improvise at least one chorus, and only use the notes in this scale:

F BLUES SCALE

➤ The F Blues scale can also be used to improvise rhythmic and melodic variations on "Latin Blues." Improvise at least one chorus, and only use the notes in this scale:

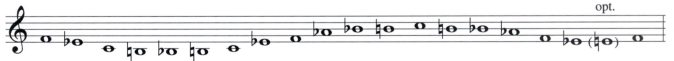

➤ Identify the scale tones of the F Blues scale which do not appear in the F Minor Pentatonic scale.

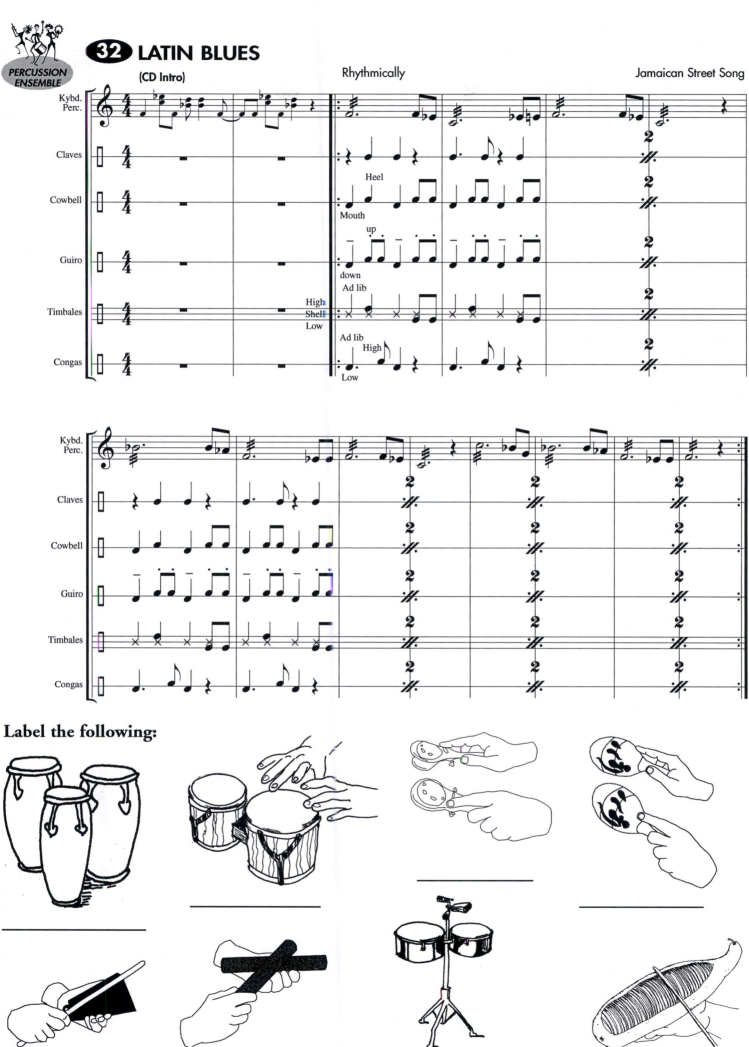

32 LATIN BLUES

(CD Intro)　　　　　　　　Rhythmically　　　　　　　Jamaican Street Song

Label the following:

33 **CHOUCOUNE (The Mocking Bird)**

Haiti

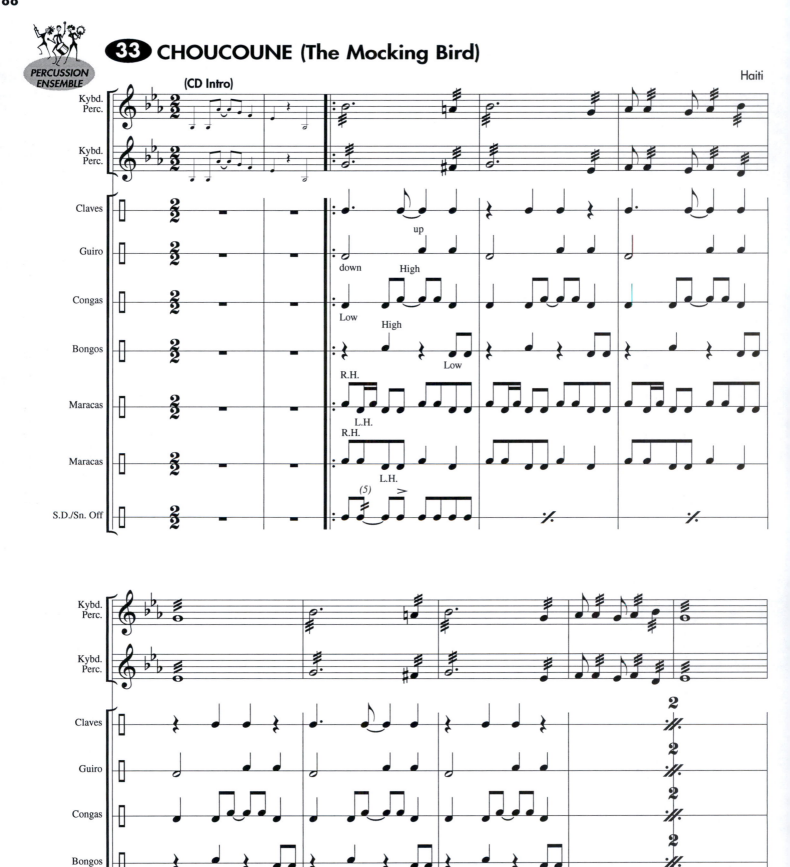

BONGOS

The Bongos originated in Cuba. They are a pair of small high-pitched drums attached side by side and held between the legs of a seated player. Attached to a stand, they can be played in a standing position. Right handed players put the smaller drum on the left. The drums are played using a combination of strokes of the fingers and thumb.

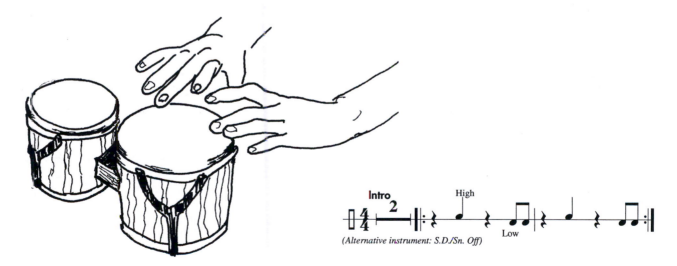

(Alternative instrument: S.D./Sn. Off)

34 HAT DANCE FROM MEXICO

BRAZILIAN

> **PORTFOLIO – Brazilian Music, Instruments, and Culture**
> The Surdo, Agogo Bells, Pandeiro, Tamborim, and Ganza are often used in Brazilian music. Find recordings of two Brazilian musicians or groups. Listen carefully to the percussion rhythms. Do you find yourself moving even while you're listening? It's impossible to play Brazilian music without dancing! How does Brazilian music compare with African music? Identify different rhythmic patterns or instruments that give Brazilian music its unique sound. What does Brazilian music say to you?

SURDO

The Surdo serves as the Brazilian bass drum. Like the marching snare drum, it is held by a sling. It is played with a beater or mallet (large head, hard felt) in combination with the hand, which is employed to dampen certain beats.

+ = dampen w/ hand
o = open

(Alternative instrument: Bass Drum)

AGOGO BELLS

The Agogo Bells consist of two differently pitched bells joined by a curved rod. It is played with a stick held in the right hand while holding the bells with the left hand, which is also free to squeeze the bells together to produce a variety of interesting sounds and rhythms.

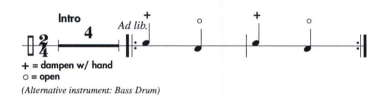

(Alternative instrument: Cowbell)

PANDEIRO

The Pandeiro is similar to the American tambourine. However, its inverted jingles produce a warmer, dryer sound. The performance technique involves three different movements:

1) **T** - strike with thumb,
2) **F** - strike with fingertips, and
3) **H** - strike with heel of hand.

(Alternative instrument: Tambourine)

TAMBORIM

The Tamborim is the smallest drum used in the Brazilian percussion ensemble (Batucada). It is a single-headed drum about 6 inches in diameter similar to a small American tambourine without jingles. It is held in the left hand at eye level and struck with a thin timbale-like stick. The best tone is produced when the head is struck slightly off center.

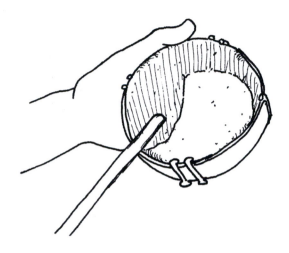

(Alternative instrument: S.D. Shell)

GANZA

The Ganza is a tubular metal shaker commonly employed in Brazilian music ensembles. It is held at eye level with both hands. The sound is produced with a forward-backward shaking motion.

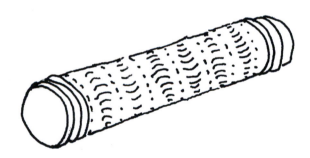

(Alternative instrument: Shaker)

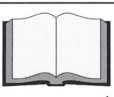

PORTFOLIO – Percussion Ensemble Arrangement

Find an African, Afro-Cuban, or Brazilian song, and write a percussion ensemble using at least four instruments often used in the corresponding country's music. Share and perform the arrangements with your class. What other historical or cultural lessons can be taught using your arrangement? Put your answers and ideas in your portfolio.

35 CHILDREN'S TUNE

➢ Improvise on all instruments with and without the CD. Enjoy!

➢ Name the musical style of this arrangement:_____

➢ Be sure to play all parts. Listen how your part fits in with others.

Label the following:

_____   _____   _____   _____

SAMBA

The Samba is a Brazilian dance music with African origins. Sambas are written in duple meter and are often written in cut time.

➤ The same Brazilian instruments and rhythms used in "Children's Tune" (Exercise 35) should be played with "Sambalele" on CD#2 Track 36. Rotate parts. The drumset plays a basic samba pattern.

36 SAMBALELE

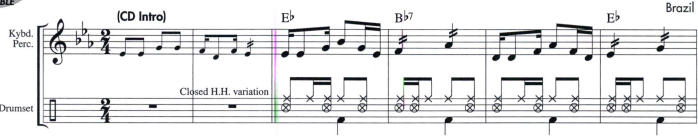

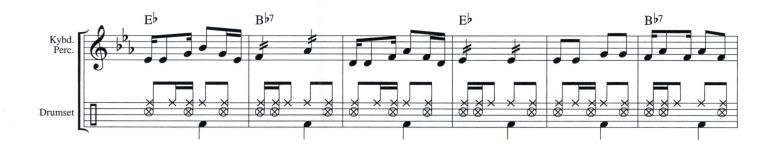

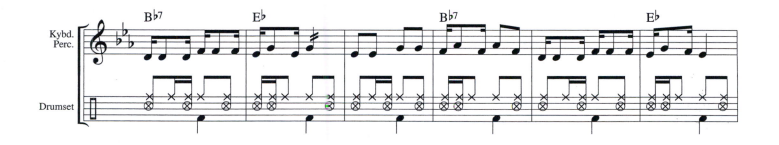

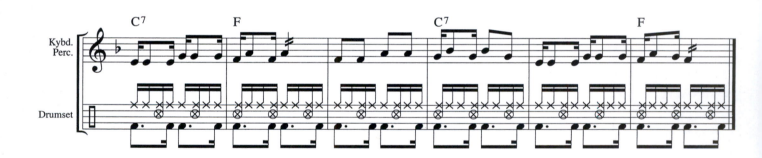

PERCUSSION
ENSEMBLE

37 EXTENDED BRAZILIAN PLAY ALONG

➤ Using the rhythms on the instruments you've learned, play along with CD#2 Track 37. Listen how these simple rhythm patterns create the unique sound of Brazilian music. Feel free to improvise rhythms.

Skills Assessment • Exercises 29 – 37

SKILLS: **This performance demonstrates:**

	10 9	8 7 6	5 4 3	2 1 0
African Styles • Play Ex. 29, 30, 31.	Correct technique on all instruments. Accurate rhythms, and accents enhance African style and musical context. Time is solid.	Rhythms are sometimes unsteady. Accents are inconsistent. Instrument is sometimes out of balance with ensemble.	Uneven rhythms, few accents, and unsteady pulse. Time and balance suffer due to lack of listening adjustment.	Inability to play African instruments correctly, or with sense of style.
Afro-Cuban Styles • Play Ex. 32, 33, 34.	Correct technique on all instruments. Accurate rhythms, and accents enhance Afro-Cuban style and musical context. Time is solid.	Rhythms are sometimes unsteady. Accents are inconsistent. Instrument is sometimes out of balance with ensemble.	Uneven rhythms, few accents, and unsteady pulse. Time and balance suffer due to lack of listening adjustment.	Inability to play Afro-Cuban instruments correctly, or with sense of style.
Brazilian Styles • Play Ex. 35, 36, 37.	Correct technique on all instruments. Accurate rhythms, and accents enhance Brazilian style and musical context. Time is solid.	Rhythms are sometimes unsteady. Accents are inconsistent. Instrument is sometimes out of balance with ensemble.	Uneven rhythms, few accents, and unsteady pulse. Time and balance suffer due to lack of listening adjustment.	Inability to play Brazilian instruments correctly, or with sense of style.
Keyboard Improvisation • Play *Latin Blues* on pg. 87 as instructed.	Improvisations include effective tension/release phrasing using correct scale notes.	Tension/release is inconsistent in improvisations. Most notes are within scales.	Improvisations lack in tension/release phrases, and do not use many correct scale notes.	Inability to perform rhythmic or harmonic improvisations using these scales.

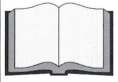

PORTFOLIO – African, Afro-Cuban, Brazilian Music
Describe the fundamental differences between African, Afro-Cuban, and Brazilian music, including different instruments used, characteristic rhythms of each instrument, etc. Write your observations in your portfolio.

Comments / Point Total:

The Marching Percussion Section

In the last century, the contemporary marching percussion section has evolved from a military time keeping section into a very important musical element of the modern marching ensemble. Most high school music programs have a marching band, so it is important as a band director to have a working knowledge of the marching percussion section. The instrumentalists in your percussion section have their own unique needs and can offer a great variety of sounds, colors, and textures that can be utilized in today's marching band if handled properly.

A QUICK OVERVIEW

The battery - This is the segment of the ensemble that plays while marching on the field. The battery is generally made up of a snare section, multi-tenor or quad section, a bass drum section and a cymbal section. The cymbal section as part of the battery provides timing for the full ensemble, support of the melodic line, and rhythmic interest in addition to a wide range of colors and dynamic contrasts.

The front ensemble or "pit" - In the late 1970s and early 1980s, drum corps and marching bands came to their senses and stopped carrying timpani and mallet keyboards on the field as part of the battery. They moved these instruments to the front sidelines at the 50 yard line and it became known as the "pit." Today, this segment is made up of the instruments that usually are not carried by the field battery. These instruments include, but are not limited to, mallet keyboards (vibes, xylophone, bells, marimba), timpani, concert bass drum and gong, chimes, sound effects, Latin percussion and drum set. In recent years, electronic keyboards, bass and percussion have become widely used, providing a wider range of color and depth to the ensemble. The pit is the "icing on the cake," providing colors that cannot be produced by any other segment of the band as well as melodic and harmonic support and rhythmic interest.

ORGANIZING A MARCHING PERCUSSION SECTION

Just as you would balance your instrumentation of your wind players, you need to balance the instrumentation of your percussion section. This is one of the keys to the success of not only your drumline, but your entire marching band. If you are limited on the number of available percussionists, you may want to consider having a battery only or a pit only. This depends on your educational philosophy and what you want your percussionists to achieve. This may be an option if you have less than ten percussionists. Here are some examples of some balanced configurations:

8 players: 1 snare, 1 quad, 3 basses, 2 keyboard, 1 auxiliary

10 players: 2 snares, 1 quad, 4 basses, 2 keyboard, 1 auxiliary

12 players: 2 snares, 2 quads, 4 basses, 2 keyboards, 1 timpani/percussion, 1 auxiliary

14 players: 3 snares, 2 quads, 4 basses, 3 keyboards, 1 timpani/percussion, 1 auxiliary

There are many variations that can be configured depending on the number of players you have available. Also consider double reed players, piano players, string players, vocalists, and wind players who can't march due to physical and health reasons in the front ensemble.

BUILDING GOOD TECHNIQUE

A percussion section needs a good basic warm-up regimen in order to perform the demands of the music on the marching field. Not only must they play well as individuals, but they must play together as an ensemble and the battery members have to play together with good technique while moving around on the field. When rehearsing with the percussion section alone, the snares should be in the middle of the battery, the tenors to either the right or left of the snares and the basses on the opposite side from the tenors facing the snares. You should have a section leader in both the battery and the pit so that the other members can listen to that person while warming up. This trains them to listen to a common point for timing and ensemble cohesiveness. The pit should warm up with the section leader in the center, preferably on xylophone, with the other players balanced on either side. The battery should stand behind the pit if the two segments are rehearsing together so that the pit can get used to listening back. Here are some examples of basic warm-ups for both front ensemble and battery:

MARCHING PERCUSSION TECHNICAL EXERCISES

8 ON A HAND

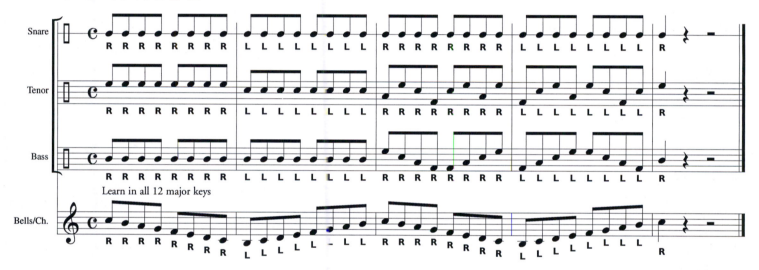

ACCENT/TAP

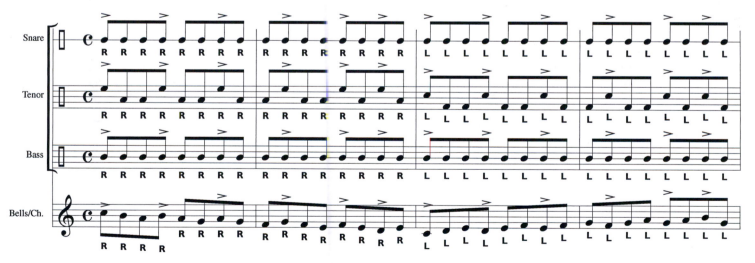

DOUBLE BEATS

ROVING ACCENTS

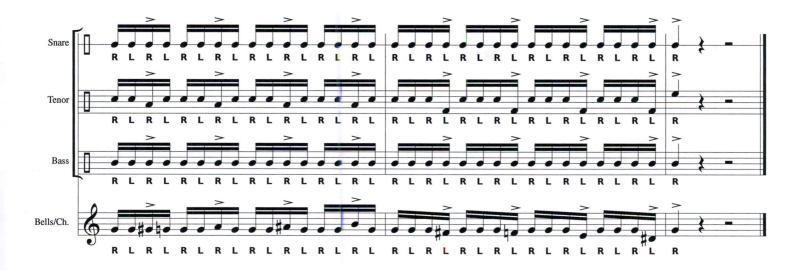

16TH PULSE ROLL SEQUENCING (Digga-Burr)

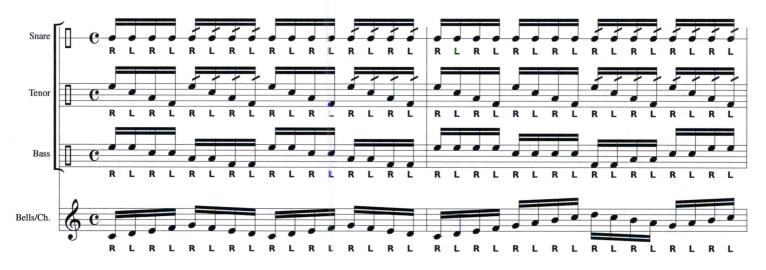

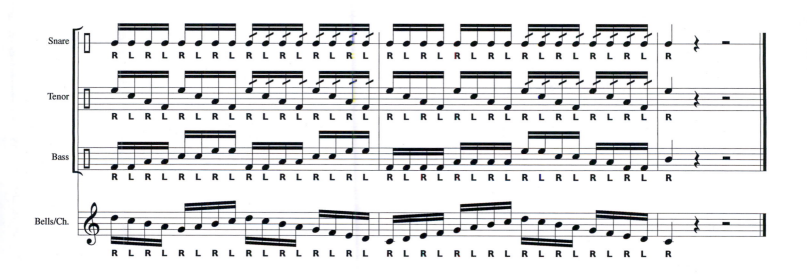

TRIPLET PULSE ROLL SEQUENCING

REHEARSING THE ENSEMBLE

Always remember that good sound production is important on any instrument whether they are being played indoors or outdoors. The same musical rules apply to your marching percussion section that apply to your indoor wind ensemble, percussion ensemble or jazz band. First of all, each individual player needs to play with good technique. Next, the individual members of the section need to listen to each other and play together. Ultimately, every section on the field must know where they need to watch and listen so that the sound they produce reaches the audience at the same time. The listening responsibility will shift while performing on the field as the drill moves and the voicing changes within the section.

Here is a general hierarchy of listening in the marching percussion section:

> The center snare watches the drum major
> The battery members listen in to the center snare
> The pit listens in to the center of the front ensemble while listening back to the battery

The pit should not watch the drum major without listening to the back ensemble. This causes many timing problems due to the properties of sound and how it travels. The pit must play with the sound of the field ensemble as it reaches them.

FIELD PLACEMENT DO'S AND DON'TS

Try to keep the battery in the same configuration as when they warm up. Avoid placing the battery on the far left or right sides of the field when they are providing timing. Almost anything goes during a battery tacet section such as a ballad. Also, avoid separating the segments of the section unless they have a lot of experience or you have a specialist that can deal with the timing issues this presents.

Place the front ensemble directly in front of the band on front sideline so that the section splits the 50 yard line. There are many different placement choices for the pit, but these can cause timing problems and should only be done if you have a specialist to help with ensemble timing.

If you have a small band, avoid placing the drumline behind the back hash marks. This can cause timing problems and balance issues that you don't need to deal with.

Avoid placing the battery in front of the winds unless they are featured.

Avoid placing the battery in a vertical line, especially at big ensemble moments.

Bass drums should face 90 degrees to the front so that one of their drum heads is always facing the audience. A good rule is to always have them face the 50 yard line.

Make sure that your pit players don't have to turn farther than 180 degrees to play an instrument. Their bodies should always face the audience if possible for maximum performance effect.

SOME GENERAL TIPS FOR MARCHING PERCUSSION

Have all of your performers play with good posture and good marching technique in the battery. This will help maximize sound quality and support good playing technique.

Proper instrument carriage and playing height are a key to good technique and sound quality. Make sure that the instruments aren't too high or too low for the performer.

Use the proper implements on all instruments.

Use the correct heads on battery percussion, timpani, concert toms, and Latin percussion. Synthetic heads are now being made for congas, bongos, and other ethnic percussion instruments to avoid the problems inherent with animal skin heads in the outdoor setting.

ONE LAST WORD...

If you can afford to bring in a percussion specialist, it is highly recommended. However, there is a downfall to be aware of with hiring a specialist. Don't let the specialist become the babysitter for your percussionists. Be actively involved with the percussion section and learn all that you can from your specialist. Chances are they won't be at every rehearsal and when you get to concert band season, you'll have to deal with them on a daily basis. Stay in control of your program and the musical direction that you would like for all of your students.

Resources

Book Title	Author (Publisher)
Championship Concepts for Marching Band	Thom Hannum (Hal Leonard)
The Rudimental Cookbook	Edward Freytag (Row-Loff)
Savage Rudimental Workshop	Matt Savage (Warner Bros.)
Quad Logic	Bill Bachman (Row-Loff)
Modern Multi-Tenor Techniques and Solos	Julie Davila (Row-Loff)
Championship Technique for Marching Percussion	James Campbell (Row-Loff)

For additional information or questions, contact www.rowloff.com

---

Special thanks to Mike Nevin of the Concord Blue Devils for his valuable assistance compiling the Marching Percussion section of this book.

Resources

Percussive Arts Society International Drum Rudiments

All rudiments should be practiced slow-fast-slow.

I. ROLL RUDIMENTS

A. SINGLE STROKE ROLL RUDIMENTS

1. SINGLE STROKE ROLL

2. SINGLE STROKE FOUR

3. SINGLE STROKE SEVEN

B. MULTIPLE BOUNCE ROLL RUDIMENTS

4. MULTIPLE BOUNCE ROLL

5. TRIPLE STROKE ROLL

C. DOUBLE STROKE OPEN ROLL RUDIMENTS

6. DOUBLE STROKE OPEN ROLL

7. FIVE STROKE ROLL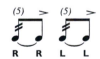

8. SIX STROKE ROLL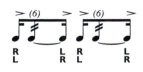

9. SEVEN STROKE ROLL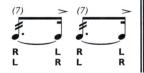

10. NINE STROKE ROLL

11. TEN STROKE ROLL

12. ELEVEN STROKE ROLL

13. THIRTEEN STROKE ROLL

14. FIFTEEN STROKE ROLL

15. SEVENTEEN STROKE ROLL

II. DIDDLE RUDIMENTS

16. SINGLE PARADIDDLE

17. DOUBLE PARADIDDLE

18. TRIPLE PARADIDDLE

19. SINGLE PARADIDDLE-DIDDLE

III. FLAM RUDIMENTS	IV. DRAG RUDIMENTS

20. FLAM

31. DRAG

21. FLAM ACCENT

32. SINGLE DRAG TAP

22. FLAM TAP

33. DOUBLE DRAG TAP

23. FLAMACUE

34. LESSON 25

24. FLAM PARADIDDLE

35. SINGLE DRAGADIDDLE

36. DRAG PARADIDDLE

25. SINGLE FLAMMED MILL

26. FLAM PARADIDDLE-DIDDLE

37. DRAG PARADIDDLE #2

27. PATAFLAFLA

38. SINGLE RATAMACUE

28. SWISS ARMY TRIPLET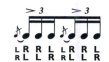

39. DOUBLE RATAMACUE

29. INVERTED FLAM TAP

40. TRIPLE RATAMACUE

30. FLAM DRAG

Percussion Instrument Alternatives

When a particular percussion instrument is not available, use an appropriate alternative. The list below may give you some ideas. Experiment with these items and others to find the best available sound.

Agogo Bells
- cowbell

Bongos
- snare drum with snares off

Castanets
- shell of drum (with snare drum sticks)
- woodblock (with snare drum sticks)

Caxixi
- rattles or maracas

Claves
- broomstick handle (cut into 6" lengths)
- clay pots
- drum sticks (large)
- woodblock (small)

Concert Bass Drum
- cardboard box (large)
- bass drum (drumset or marching)
- sheet of cardboard (large)

Congas
- high drum and low drum

Cowbell
- dome of cymbal (with butt or shank or drum stick)

Dawuro (African Bell)
- cowbell

Djembe
- high drum and low drum

Djun-Djun
- bass drum

Finger cymbals
- triangle
- crown of cymbal with small metal beater
- metal washers (large, with string handles)

Gankogui (African Double Bell)
- temple blocks

Ganza
- shaker

Guiro
- snare drum rim

Maracas
- shakers (large)
- lemon or lime juice bulbs (filled with rice, with pencil handle)
- wooden boxes filled with small pebbles, beads, rice, or dry beans

Metal Beater
- large nail
- metal fork

Pandeiro
- tambourine

Shekere
- maracas

Sleigh Bells
- "jingle belt" (with metal buttons, jingles, rings, or washers attached through holes in belt)
- headless tambourine

Surdo
- bass drum

Suspended Cymbal
- baking sheet
- metal pot cover (large)
- hand cymbal (suspended or hand held)

Tamborim
- snare drum shell

Tambourine
- embroidery hoop (with metal buttons, jingles, rings, or washers attached whrough holes in belt)

Temple Blocks
- woodblocks (assorted sizes)
- wooden salad bowl set
- empty cans (assorted sizes)
- wooden chairs (assorted sizes)

Timbales
- snare drum shell with snares off

Triangle
- bell of cymbal (with metal beater)
- glass or mug (high-pitched)
- pan lid (small; glass or metal)

Wire Brushes
- pastry brushes
- whiskbroom

Woodblock
- wooden chair back
- wooden desk top
- temple block (high)
- wooden shell of bass drum

Suggested Methods

The following is a list of books that represent the most effective and popular books in each category. Many of the books are at the beginning level. (*)

SNARE DRUM

Primary Handbook for Snare Drum by Garwood Whaley *
Stick Control by George Lawrence Stone
Modern Rudimental Swing Solos by Charley Wilcoxson
Portraits in Rhythm by Anthony Cirone
Stick Twisters by Buster Bailey

MALLETS

Primary Handbook for Mallets by Garwood Whaley *
Fundamental Method for Mallets by Mitchell Peters *
Modern School for Xylophone, Marimba and Xylophone by Morris Goldenberg

TIMPANI

Primary Handbook for Timpani by Garwood Whaley *
Fundamental Method for Timpani by Mitchell Peters *
Modern Method for Timpani by Saul Goodman *
The Solo Timpanist by Vic Firth
Exercises, Etudes, and Solos for the Timpani by Raynor Carroll

CONCERT PERCUSSION

Cymbals: A Crash Course by Mitchell Peters
Modern School for Snare Drum by Morris Goldenberg
The Logic of it All by Anthony Cirone
Orchestral Repertoire for Bass Drum and Cymbals by Raynor Caroll
The Art of Tambourine and Triangle Playing by Neil Grover and Garwood Whaley
The Art of Percussion Accessory Playing by Anthony Cirone and Garwood Whaley

DRUMSET

Beginner...

My First Drumset Book by Steve Houghton and Dave Black *
Sessions by Peter O. Gorman *
Drumset Performer by Steve Houghton *

Jazz...

The Art of Bop Drumming by John Riley
The Drumset Soloist by Steve Houghton

Latin...

Brazilian Techniques for Drumset by Maria Martinez
Afro-Cuban Techniques for Drumset by Maria Martinez

Funk-Rock...

Future Sounds by David Garibaldi
The Funky Beat by David Garibaldi

Style Compilations

Essential Styles (Books 1 and 2) by Steve Houghton *

Reading

Studio and Big Band Drumming by Steve Houghton *
Big Band Primer by Ed Soph
The Ultimate Drumset Reading Anthology by Steve Houghton

Technique

Advanced Technique for the Modern Drummer by Jim Chapin *
Essential Technique for Drumset by Ed Soph
Patterns, Vol. III Time Functioning by Gary Chaffee

Brushes

The Sound of Brushes by Ed Thigpen

WORLD PERCUSSION

World Music Drumming by Will Schmid
Play Congas Now – The Basics and Beyond by Richie Gajate-Garcia
Show Me the Rhythms by Kalani (Video series)
Have Fun Playing Hand Drums by Kalani (Video & book series)

RESOURCE GUIDES

The Complete Percussionist by Bob Breithaupt
Teaching Percussion by Gary Cook
Percussion Education: A Source Book of Concepts and Information by PAS
Percussion Repair and Maintenance by Mark Bonfoey

For all your percussion needs, visit www.pas.org

Stick and Mallet Choices for Percussionists

Choosing the proper mallet for an instrument involves several aspects.

One must remember the following general rules about all mallets and beaters:

- Above all else, strive to make the best possible sound, no matter the instrument, the music or the environment. Quality of sound is foremost.

- The harder the mallet, the greater the articulation; the softer the mallet, the greater the tone.

- A large membrane or surface requires a larger, more massive mallet and a smaller membrane or surface requires a smaller mallet.

- Volume is not determined by only the hardness of the mallet in most cases.

- Improper choice and use of mallets will produce a poor quality sound and can damage the instrument.

- There is no one perfect mallet for every player, every instrument and/or every piece of music.

- While some mallets will be useful in both concert band and marching settings, not all will. Always be sensitive to the music and tone quality.

- Creativity and sensitivity must be used when choosing the proper mallet to create the desired color from the instrument.

- Whenever possible, purchase the highest quality mallets and sticks.

- Don't hesitate to experiment and try something new.

When deciding on a mallet choice within a musical selection, one must be aware of these aspects:

- is the musical role of the part more rhythmic, melodic, or harmonic;
- is the musical role soloistic or supportive;
- should the desired sound blend or contrast with the other instruments;
- how much projection is needed and/or desired;
- what mallet choice is indicated by the composer/arranger and is it the best choice.
- don't accept a poor quality of sound due to a lack of mallet selection. Any great craftsman or sportsman has the proper tools to do the job (i.e. carpenter, plumber, golfer, hunter).

By combining all of these ideas, correct choices can be made regarding mallet selection that will produce a beautiful sound that is integral to the musical selection while maintaining the life of the instrument. Remember: Be SENSITIVE, CREATIVE, and EXCITED!

Note: Most stick and mallet manufacturers have developed concise, understandable mallet selection guides, which should make the band director's job easier.

Used with permission of David L. Collier, Illinois State University.

Example 3:44 *Mallet Selection Chart* †

MALLET TYPE	BELLS	SYNTHETIC XYLOPHONE	ROSEWOOD XYLOPHONE	VIBRAPHONE	SYNTHETIC MARIMBA	ROSEWOOD MARIMBA	CHIMES	CROTALES	KEYBOARD CONTROLLER
BRASS	●								
ALUMINUM	●							●	
PLASTIC	●						●	●	
ACRYLIC/POLY	●	●					●	●	
ROSEWOOD		●	●						
HARD RUBBER	●	●	●		●				
MEDIUM RUBBER		●	●		●	●			
SOFT RUBBER			●	●	●	●			
CORD WRAPPED				●	●	●			●
YARN WRAPPED				●	●	●			●
RAWHIDE HAMMER							●		
ACRYLIC HAMMER							●		

† From the text, "The Complete Percussionist," Robert Breithaupt. Published by C. L. Barnhouse. Used with permission.

Percussion Manufacturers Directory

American Drum Manufacturing
Phone: 303-722-3844
Fax: 303-722-3025
Post Office Box 40403
Denver, Colorado 80204
www.americandrum-w-light.com
comments@americandrum-w-light.com

Axis Percussion
24416 South Main Street
Suite 311
Carson, California 90745
Phone 800-457-3630
Fax 310- 549-7728
www.axispercussion.com

Ayotte Drums Inc.
2060 Pine Street,
Vancouver, British Columbia
Canada V6J 4P8
Telephone: Toll-free in North America:
(877) 736-5111
Outside North America: (604) 736-5411
Fax: (604) 736-9411
info@ayottedrums.com

Bergerault Percussion
B.P 2 Route de Ferrière
37 240 Ligueil, France
0033(0)2 47 59 94 59
0033(0)2 47 92 06 79
percussions@bergerault.com

BlackSwamp Percussion LLC
13493 New Holland St., Suite E
Holland, MI 49424 USA
Tel: 616-738-3190
Fax: 616-738-3105
www.blackswamp.com
info@blackswamp.com

Brady Drum Company Pty. Ltd.
17 Stone Street
Armadale, WA 6112
Australia
Phone +61 8 9497 2212
Fax +61 8 9497 2242
www.bradydrums.com
info@bradydrums.com.au

Clevelander Drum Company
3800 Kelley Ave.
Cleveland, OH 44114
Phone: 800-321-0556
Fax: 216-391-8999
www.cmigroup.org
drum@grotro.com

Fall Creek Marimbas
PO Box 118
1445 Upper Hill Road
Middlesex, NY 14507
Phone: 585-554-4011
Fax: 585-554-4017
www.marimbas.com
bill@marimbas.com

**Grover Pro Percussion, Inc. -
Grover Pro, Silverfox,
Spectrasound**
22 Prospect Street, Unit 7
Woburn, MA 01801, U.S.A.
Phone (781) 935-6200
Fax (781) 935-5522
www.groverpro.com
email@groverpro.com

HQ Percussion Products
P.O. Box 430065
St. Louis, MO 63143 USA
PHONE: (314) 647-9009
FAX: (314) 644-0097
www.hqpercussion.com
HQpercussion@aol.com

Innovative Percussion Inc.
470 Metroplex Drive, Ste. 214
Nashville, TN 37211
Phone (615) 333-9388
Fax (615) 333-9354
www.innovativepercussion.com
info@innovativepercussion.com

**Kaman Music Corporation -
Gibralter, Toca, LP, Gretsch
Drums, Drum Frame**
PO Box 507
Bloomfield, CT 06002-0507
www.kamanmusic.com
info@kamanmusic.com

Kori Percussion
www.custommusiccorp.com

Lark In The Morning
PO Box 799
Fort Bragg, CA 95437
USA
Phone (707) 964-5569
Fax (707) 964-1979
www.larkinam.com
Support@larkinam.com

Latin Percussion, Inc.
160 Belmont Avenue
Garfield, NJ 07026 USA
973-478-6903
www.lpmusic.com

**Ludwig - Musser / A div of The
Selmer Company**
P.O. Box 310
Elkhart, Indiana 46515-0310
www.ludwig-drums.com

Majestic Percussion
Communicatielaan 6-8
NL-8466 SR NIJEHASKE
THE NETHERLANDS
Telephone: (+31) 513 46 80 30
Fax number: (+31) 513 46 80 31
www.majestic-percussion.com
info@majestic-percussion.com

Malletech Instruments
c/o kp3
www.mostlymarimba.com

Malletech Mallets
P.O. Box 467,
Asbury Park, NJ 07712

Marimba One
PO Box 767
Arcata, CA 95518
Phone 888 990 6663
Fax 707 822 6256
www.marimba1.com
Percussion@marimba1.com

MEINL Cymbals & Percussion
a division of Roland Meinl
Musikinstrumente GmbH & Co. KG
Am Bahnhof 2
91468 Gutenstetten Germany
Phone: 49 - (0) 9161 - 6625 - 0
Fax: 49 - (0) 9161 - 6625 - 25
www.meinl.de
csger@meinl.de

Mike Balter Mallets, LLC
15 E. Palatine Rd. Suite 116
Prospect Heights, IL 60070
USA Phone: 847.541.5777
Fax: 847.541.5785
www.mikebalter.com
info@mikebalter.com

Paiste Cymbals
www.paiste.com

**Pearl Corporation/
Adams Percussion**
100 Metroplex Drive
Nashville TN
800-947-3275
www.pearldrums.com

Percussion Construction
P.O. Box 876
Arkadelphia, AR 71923
Phone 800-362-5538
Fax (870) 403-0864
www.percussionconstruction.com
sales@percussionconstruction.com

**The Percussion Source - Freer
Percussion, Chronos, A. Stubbs
Percussion, Buddy & Thein, David
Roman Drums, Enbloc, Heidler
Drums, Schiedmayer Celesta**
1212 Fifth St
Coralville, IA 52241
Phone 866/849-4387
Fax 888/470-3942
www.percussionsource.com
Service@percussionsource.com

Pork Pie Percussion(tm)
72411/2 Eton Ave,
Canoga Park, CA 91303
Phone: (818) 992-0783
Fax: (818) 992-1358
www.westworld.com/~porkpie
porkpie@westworld.com

Pro-Mark Corporation
11550 Old Main Street
Houston, TX 77025
Phone 800.233.5250
Fax 713.669.8000
www.promarkdrumsticks.com
Info@promarkdrumsticks.com

Remo Inc.
28101 Industry Drive
Valencia, CA 91355
Tel: 661-294-5600
www.remo.com
customerservice@remo.com

Ross Percussion Products
www.ross.com

Sabian Cymbals
Meductic, NK CANADA E0H 1L0

Salazar Fine Tuning
P.O. Box 509
Arcata, California 95518 USA
www.salazarfinetuning.com
Info@salazarfinetuning.com

Slug Percussion Products
Box 578306
Chicago, IL 60657-8306 USA
Phone: 312-432-0553 .
Fax: 312-432-0552
www.slugdrums.com
webmaster@slugdrums.com

Vater Percussion
270 Centre Street
Unit D
Holbrook, MA 02343 USA
Phone: 781-767-1877
Fax: 781-767-0010
www.vater.com
vaterinc@aol.com

Vic Firth, Incorporated
65 Commerce Way
Dedham, MA 02026-2953 U.S.A.
Telephone: 781-326-3455
Fax: 781-326-1273
www.vicfirth.com
Info@vicfirth.com

**XL Specialty Percussion -
Protechtor and Elite Air cases**
P.O. Box 70
Grabill, IN 46741
Phone 800-348-1012
Fax 260-627-8077
www.xlspec.com
xlspec@mixi.net

Yamaha Musical Products
6600 Orangethorpe Ave.
Buena Park, CA 90620
714-522-9011
FAX:714-522-9475
www.yamaha.com

Avedis Zildjian Co.
(cymbals, sticks and mallets)
22 Longwater Drive
Norwell, MA. 02061
800-229-8672
www.zildjian.com

Percussion Publishers Directory

Alfred Publishing
www.alfred.com

Advance Music
www.advancemusic.com

Batterie Music
Battmusik@aol.com

Berklee Press
www.berkleepress.com

C Alan Publications
www.c-alanpublications.com

Carl Fischer
www.carlfischer.com

Cherry Lane Music
www.musicdispatch.com

C.L. Barnhouse
www.Barnhouse.com

Colgrass Music
www.carlfischer.com

Editions Musicales Alphonse Leduc
www.alphonseleduc.com

GIA Publications
www.giamusic.com

GK Music Co
www.GK-Music.com

Hal Leonard Corporation
www.musicdispatch.com

Hudson Music
www.hudsonmusic.com

J.R. Publications
www.dumontmusic.com

Kendor Music, Inc.
www.kendormusic.com

Keyboard Percussion Publications
Kpp@mostlymarimba.com

Klavier Music Productions
www.klavier-records.com

Ludwig Music Publishing Co.
www.ludwigmusic.com

MalletWorks Media
www.malletworks.com

Mandara Music Productions
www.mardaramusic.com

Marimba Productions
Kpp@mostlymarimba.com

Media Press, Inc.
Siwe@ux1.cso.uiuc.edu

Mel Bay Publications
www.melbay.com

Meredith Music Publications
www.musicdispatch.com

Modern Drummer Publications
www.halleonard.com

Multicultural Media
www.worldmusicstore.com

Neil Kjos Music Company
www.kjos.com

Per-Mus Publications
www.Permus@aol.com

Playin' Time Productions Inc.
www.carlfischer.com

Really Good Music
www.reallygoodmusic.com

Roland Music
www.rolandvazquez.com

Row-Loff Productions
www.rowloff.com

Sam Ulano
www.samulano.com

Sierra Music
Ph. 509-255-9928

Stanley Leonard Percussion Music
slpercmu@aol.com

Studio 4
www.alfred.com

Tap Space Publications
www.tapspace.com

Touchdown Productions
Fax – 323-478-9938

Warner Bros. Publications
www.warnerbrospublications.com

William L. Cahn Publishing
Ph. 716-582-2508

Do It!
Play in Band
A Beginning Band Method

James O. Froseth

Contributing editors: Marguerite Wilder and Molly A. Weaver

Co-author, Percussion: Steve Houghton

Co-author, Strings: Bret Smith

This major new band method by James O. Froseth has it all:

- Artist performers set musical standards in sound with more than 80 great performances on CD for every instrument!

- Professional studio backgrounds capture the rich diversity of American music culture with a repertoire of American, Latin American, African, European, and Far Eastern styles.

- Music from the 12th-century to jazz, blues, and rock-and-roll.

- Every song includes text, providing information about phrasing, rhythm, style, affect, emotion, history, and culture.

- A unique Rhythmic Pattern Dictionary allows students to "look it up" and "listen up."

- An individualized format allows students to progress at different rates with a "theme and variation" format.

- Ear training and improvisation are integral parts of the lesson format.

- A 550+ page teacher's resource edition and musical score provides options galore, including a double CD with "listen and play" exercises for group instruction, supplementary exercises for technical development, and resource material for improvisation and composition. All the resources needed for teaching to the National Standards for Music.

- Book 2 features innovative use of world percussion instruments, as developed by percussion educator Steve Houghton.

INSTRUMENT	Bk 1 & CD	Bk 2 & CD
Flute	M454	M494
Clarinet	M450	M496
Bass Clarinet	M450	M496
Alto Clarinet	M492	M498
Oboe	M458	M500
Bassoon	M461	M502
Alto Sax	M464	M504
Baritone Sax	M464	M504
Tenor Sax	M467	M506
Trumpet	M470	M508
Horn in F	M473	M510
Trombone	M476	M512
Baritone TC	M491	M514
Baritone BC	M479	M516
Tuba	M482	M518
Percussion (Double book)	M485	M520
Teacher's Resource Edition Full Score, & CDs for Band	M486	M523

Recorder:
Recorder Book & CD	M438 M437 (book only) M436 (CD only)
Teacher's Resource Edition for Recorder with Two CDs	M441
GIA Heavy-Duty Soprano Recorder	M447
Book, CD, Recorder	M440
Violin	M526

Do It!
Play Violin

Strings:
Viola	M527
Cello	M528
Bass	M529
Teacher's Resource Strings with Three CDs	M530

GIA Publications, Inc.
1.800.442.1358 • www.giamusic.com

Do It! Play World Percussion.

**African
World Percussion**

**Brazilian
World Percussion**

**Afro-Cuban
World Percussion**

African Package

qty.	model	description
1	DJ-0012-PM	12" Djembé (KinteKloth)
1	DJ-0014-PM	14" Djembé (KinteKloth)
1	E1-1922-A4	22" Djun-Djun (Forest Green)
1	E1-2116-A4	16" Djun-Djun (Forest Green)
4	SR-0235-00	2" Shaker (KinteKloth)
1	CW-3007-VH	7" Valencia Bongo Bell
1	29-2420-05	Gongokui (Double Bell)
1	29-2420-07	Shekeré

#PP-WMDC-FF

Afro-Cuban Package

qty.	model	description
1	TU-1112-PM	12" Tubano (KinteKloth)
1	TU-1110-PM	10" Tubano (KinteKloth)
2	TU-FELG-13	Lg. Festival Tubano (Twinings)
1	CW-3007-VH	7" Valencia Bongo Bell
1	BG-5300-70	6/7" Bongos (Black)
1	TB-1314-AC	13/14" Timbacos (Black)
1	29-2420-02	Guiro w/stick
1	29-2420-04	Maracas
1	29-2420-03	Claves

#PP-WMDC-HH

Brazilian Package

qty.	model	description
1	SU-3418-10	18" Surdo (Chrome)
1	SU-3816-10	16" Surdo (Chrome)
1	AG-2045-VA	Valencia Agogo Bells
1	SR-0235-00	2" Shaker (KinteKloth)
1	SR-0335-00	3" Shaker (KinteKloth)
1	TM-7206-47	6" Tamborim (Black Prizmatic)
1	PD-8110-58	10" Pandeiro (Cherry Red)
1	TM-3015-70	Baqueta

#PP-WMDC-GG

Remo, Inc.
28101 Industry Drive • Valencia, CA 91355 • USA

**The World's Drum Company
remo.com**

About the Authors

Internationally renowned jazz drummer, percussionist, clinician, author, and educator, **Steve Houghton** initially received acclaim at age twenty as the drummer with Woody Herman's Young Thundering Herd. Since then he has shared stage and studio with luminaries Diana Krall, Toots Thielemans, Christian McBride, Toshiko Akiyoshi, Freddie Hubbard, Lyle Mays, Billy Childs, Pat LaBarbara, Arturo Sandoval, Joe Henderson, and Maureen McGovern, with whom he tours today.

As band leader Houghton's discography includes: *The Manne We Love: Gershwin Revisited* (TNC), a recent release of John Williams' charts for big band and quintet, initially recorded by Shelly Manne on Capitol in 1965, the *Steve Houghton Quintet Live @ the Senator* (Jazz Compass), *Windsong* (SHPERC Records), *Remembrances* (Warner Bros.), and *Steve Houghton Signature* (Mesa-Bluemoon). In total, Houghton attributes more than one hundred recordings to his credit as a participating artist. As a classical percussionist, Houghton has performed with the Boston, and Philadelphia Pops orchestras, as well as the Hollywood Bowl Orchestra. He frequently appears as a soloist with numerous orchestras and wind ensembles throughout the world.

As author, Houghton's publications boast more than twenty composite educational tools including *Jazz Director's Guide to the Rhythm Section* (Alfred Publications), *The Ultimate Drumset Chart Reading Anthology* (Alfred), *Play and Teach Percussion* (GIA), and *The Drumset Soloist* (Warner Bros.). In addition, Houghton was recently featured in an article published in the Modern Drummer (2003) entitled "The Thundering Drummers of Woody Herman."

Houghton is currently Associate Professor of Percussion at Indiana University-Bloomington, and is on faculty at the Henry Mancini Institute. In addition to his academic duties, he presents yearly clinics and masterclasses to students around the world. Chair of The Resource Team of the International Association of Jazz Education, and board member of the Percussive Arts Society, Houghton endorses Pearl drums, Adams percussion, Zildjian cymbals, sticks, and mallets, and Remo World Percussion products and drumheads.

Linda Petersen is the Director of Programs for the Wisconsin School Music Association (WSMA), a position she has held since 1994. Her responsibilities include coordinating all aspects of the WSMA State Honors Music Project, a nationally-known program of excellence for Wisconsin's most talented student musicians. She also manages the WSMA Music Festival List including more than 5,000 carefully selected titles, the WSMA State Marching Band Championships, the WSMA/DPI Student Composition Project, is a Conference Operations Director for the Wisconsin State Music Conference, and serves on many WSMA committees. A strong believer in using specific, measurable skills in music education, she helped write rubrics for WSMA Solo & Ensemble events, and the WSMA Middle Level and High School State Honors Music Projects.

Prior to coming to WSMA, Linda was Instrumental Methods Editor, author, and clinician for Hal Leonard Corporation in Milwaukee, Wisconsin; Band Music Editor for the Neil A. Kjos Music Company in San Diego, California; and taught instrumental and vocal music in Wisconsin at the elementary, middle school, and high school levels. She was the editorial director and co-author of the *Essential Elements Comprehensive Band Method*, published by Hal Leonard. Linda is the author of the accompanying *Teacher Resource Kit*, also published by Hal Leonard. She has been an instrumental music clinician at more than 40 state, regional, and national music conventions, and has presented successful workshops in Japan, Hong Kong, England, Canada, and Australia. Recently, she collaborated with Steve Houghton on *Play and Teach Percussion*, a comprehensive percussion course for college music majors and current music teachers, published by GIA Publications.

Linda earned her Bachelor of Music Education degree with honors from the University of Wisconsin-Eau Claire, and also completed coursework at St. Olaf College in Northfield, Minnesota. In 1996, she was inducted into the Racine Washington Park High School Hall of Fame as one of 131 inductees chosen from more than 65,000 graduates, and is one of the youngest Park Hall of Fame members ever to be inducted. Linda is a member of MENC: The National Association for Music Education, NFIMA (the National Federation of Interscholastic Music Associations), serves on the Wisconsin Choral Directors Association Board of Directors, and several other board and committee positions in Wisconsin.

Index

U-Z